DIVIDED
We Fail

DIVIDED
We Fail

Issues of Equity in American Schools

Crystal M. England

HEINEMANN
Portsmouth, NH

KH

Heinemann
A division of Reed Elsevier Inc.
361 Hanover Street
Portsmouth, NH 03801–3912
www.heinemann.com

Offices and agents throughout the world

The author and publisher wish to thank those who have generously given permission to reprint borrowed material:

Untitled poem on pp. 74–75 written by author.
Students appearing in the cover photographs: Jimmie Doss and Daimontra Brown (top), Carole Anne Holbrook (insert), Rodney Harris, Quinton Wade, and Tanisha Harris (bottom), and Gladys Veronica Albarran (back cover).

Credits continue on p. vi.

Library of Congress Cataloging-in-Publication Data
England, Crystal M.
    Divided we fail : issues of equity in American schools / Crystal M. England.
        p. cm.
    Includes bibliographical references.
    ISBN 0-325-00723-3 (alk. paper)
    1. Educational equalization—United States. 2. Minorities—Education—United States. 3. Multicultural education—United States. I. Title.

LC213.2.E54 2005
379.2'6—dc22   2004020393

Acquisition Editor: Lois Bridges
Editor: Danny Miller
Production: Lynne Costa
Cover design: Joni Doherty
Cover photographs: Steve Orel
Typesetter: Tom Allen/Pear Graphic Design
Manufacturing: Steve Bernier

Printed in the United States of America on acid-free paper
09 08 07 06 05   DA   1 2 3 4 5

1/28/08

*To Mom and Dad . . . for cultivating open-mindedness
and to Alexander . . . for the character you bring to the world*

Contents

Acknowledgments

I'D LIKE TO EXPRESS MY GRATITUDE TO THE PEOPLE IN MY LIFE WHO encourage my dreams—Kristin, Randy, Ken, and Trish, you are much appreciated. A special thank you goes out to Jim—you encourage my dreams and love me because of (and in spite of) them.

The staff at Heinemann is amazing. It takes many people to bring a book to publication. Thank you to Lois Bridges, who began this journey with me, and to Danny Miller, who is finishing it, and to Lynne Costa, Doria Turner, Pat Carls, and Janet Taylor, who do so much to assist in the success of each author.

Thank you to the participants of the ACT NOW 2003 (Advocates of Children and Teachers National Organizing Workshop) Yahoo newsgroup. This group of individuals is dedicated to reform and zealous about truly caring for students. More information can be found at http://groups.yahoo.com/group/ ACTNOW2003/.

Finally, I'd like to thank Steve Orel, cofounder and director of the World of Opportunity (WOO) educational and job readiness program in Birmingham, Alabama; Corey Howard, Assistant Director and the student-authors who shared their insights in many of the boxed sections in Chapter 1. The following WOO students have shared their talent, their wisdom, and their hearts: Chris, Tieitka, Amanda, Ebony, Jamyra, Carole Anne, Samuel, Bryant, Shalicia, April, Latisha, Camika, Nicole, Candace, Jasmine, Shondria, LaWanda, Emmett, Alejandra, Katina, Frank, Cecil, Jennifer, and LaTanya. For more information on the WOO, please visit http://www.worldofopportunitywoo.org.

Introduction

IMAGINE STANDING IN A LONG LINE AT THE GROCERY STORE. YOUR cart is heaped with necessary items. You are incredulous at the number of people who also chose to shop on this hot summer day. You mop at your neck with a tissue that you dug from the deep recesses of your pocket. The store's air-conditioning seems to be working only intermittently, if, indeed, it is working at all. You watch with dismay as the person ahead of you begins to slowly sort through a wallet jammed to overflowing with coupons. You roll your eyes and then try to hide your impatience as the overwhelmed clerk turns on the bright white light above her register, calling wearily for a price check over the store's antique loudspeaker. Her voice crackles and you wince. Everything seems to be irritating in a line that doesn't move. You give a nervous glance at the ice cream that is sweating in the bottom corner of your cart. You swipe again at the perspiration that has accumulated on your brow in the seemingly endless amount of time that you've been standing, unmoving, in the grocery store line.

Suddenly, another customer approaches the registers. You note with sympathy that his cart, too, is overflowing. You see one of the clerks rise up quickly from behind the customer service desk and rush over to open the line next to yours. Just as you angle your cart in the direction of the newly opened line, you feel the store manager's hand on your shoulder, restraining you, preventing you from making progress. "I'm sorry," you are told, "but that line is just for Mr.

Jones." You are angry and insulted. You inquire about the reasons for this unfair treatment. The store manager mutters something about Mr. Jones living in the neighborhood before he beats a hasty, smiling retreat to the back of the store. You cast an angry glance at Mr. Jones, taking in his Armani suit. You wonder if that is a Rolex that you see circling his wrist. You wonder if money is what it takes to get preferential treatment in this store.

Your line begins to move again but you are fuming. If you didn't need these groceries so badly, you'd leave this store altogether. You'll certainly never patronize it again, although the other grocery store is located at the farthest end of the suburb from your home. Finally, you are unloading your groceries onto the conveyor belt. You begin to relax. You notice that your ice cream feels squishy and liquid. You inform the clerk that you don't want it, but she tells you that she must give it to you. She suggests that you try to refreeze it when you get home. Just as you are about to tell her that this is ridiculous, she pulls the Granny Smith apples from your cart and refuses to sell them to you. She hands them to a bagger and instructs him to reshelve them. When you raise your voice at such unfair treatment, she holds up her hand in a gesture of patient forbearance. She says that she can tell by a number of factors that she has been trained to recognize that Granny Smith apples will only upset your stomach. Amazed, you flee the store, certain that you have entered the Twilight Zone and that soon you will awaken in your comfortable bed, the grocery store experience the by-product of a bad dream.

The situation described above is a case of obvious inequity. Consumers do not expect to be told what they may or may not purchase. Members of a community do not expect preferential treatment within service organizations. Civilized adults have been coached since kindergarten on the merits of waiting a turn, sharing with one another, and in trying to be fair. Our legal system is based upon a system of equity so strong that it has carried our country through numerous litigious challenges throughout the last two hundred years. Justice and equality seem to be the American ideal.

But are they? Transfer your image of the grocery store to a public school. Or to several public schools. In one school, there are no lines. Affluence seems to influence education. The students are well dressed. The parents are involved. The teachers are relaxed. In another school, the classroom is crowded. Parents work several jobs to keep their families afloat financially. Some students seem tired. Some teachers seem stressed. There isn't time to provide all of the curriculum necessary because there are so many pressing basic needs to be met first. The Granny Smith apples go back on the shelf. It is obvious based upon the observation of several factors that they do not fit into some students' educational carts.

Equity is important in all facets of life. This book is dedicated to the issue of educational equity. The carrot-and-stick reform efforts of the federal government are masked as standards and assessments. But they are really carrots and sticks. Punitive efforts will effect short-term token change, but, in the end, some children will get all the carrots and some will be left clutching only sticks. It does not have to be this way. Quantifiable, reliable educational research has pointed out the direction that future practice must take in order to level the instructional field for all learners. Real reform using standards, assessments, and instructional strategies is not only possible, it is critical. When real learning is taking place, there will be no need for sticks. There won't really be a need for carrots, either. But at least we'll all still be able to purchase them at our local grocery stores.

Throughout this book on equity in America's schools, the focus will be upon educational justice. Author Edmund Gordon's words on social justice will serve as a guide for our reflection on providing equality to all American youth. In *Education and Justice: A View from the Back of the Bus,* Gordon states, "We have tended to think of social justice as a value that we are morally committed to pursue for the underprivileged, for ethnic minorities, or for any low-status group.

I argue that the absence of justice is more than a moral problem. It is a plague on the houses of all of us. It is incompatible with the purposes of education. It is a threat to the economic and political stability of the society."[1]

As Gordon alludes, justice is not a universal necessity only with regard to race. In this book, the ideas of educational equity will be examined along a full spectrum of issues inherent in societal diversity: race, economic status, and learning style. Additionally, the impact of inequity on political measures such as standards, assessments, and the No Child Left Behind Act will be discussed. Finally, the curricular relevance of equity issues will be highlighted and strategies for infusing best practices into core curricular areas will be shared.

Equity and respect are interrelated and ultimately interchangeable concepts. They are the foundations for justice and for learning. All social institutions, including America's schools, must be built upon them. Lack of respect, though less aggressive than an outright insult, can take an equally wounding form. No insult is offered another person, but neither is recognition extended. He or she is not *seen* as a full human being whose presence matters.

When a society treats the mass of people in this way, singling out only a few for recognition, it creates a scarcity of respect, as though there were not enough of this precious substance to go around. Like many famines, this scarcity is man-made, and unlike food, respect costs nothing. Why, then, should it be in short supply?[2]

CHAPTER ONE

Inequity Within Diversity

*Each of us writes at last the kind of book that we must
write, and wins the kinds of allies that we need, deserve
or yearn for.*

—*Jonathan Kozol[1]*

And We're Off!

RACE. CONSIDER THE WORD *RACE*. ONE SYLLABLE. IT GLIDES OFF
the tongue. In the minds of many it conjures up images of pumping
hearts, rapid pulses, and the excitement of attaining a final common
goal. Of winning. Of triumphing over the competition. Or perhaps
race is not a physical endeavor at all. Perhaps it is the check box on
the census form that stratifies and quantifies America by color or creed.

Next, ponder the word *diversity*. More syllables. It often causes
a cacophony of confusion when it meets the ear. A vision of the muddy
waters of difference. Does diversity refer to the colors of the rainbow—
separate but interrelated toward an overall effect? Or does it refer to
the right wing and the left wing and the myriad personalities that
gather on the bell-shaped curve that we call civilization?

And then there's *culture*. Culture raises images of ethnicity. Of
Archie Bunker row houses. Culture inspires visions of Italian restaurants and Irish wakes. Culture relies on tradition, on unique religious
practices, on exclusive inner knowledge of clothing or dialect or
uncommon holiday customs.

Race. Diversity. Culture. These are just three words that we commonly use to discuss issues of equity in America. But real equity involves so much more. *The American Heritage Dictionary*[2] defines equity as "the quality of being just." It would follow then that conditions of inequity are conditions of injustice. And statistical conditions of inequity abound.

Sonia Nieto, author of the book *Affirming Diversity,* uses the term "hyphenated American" to discuss issues of language within the United States. She states that in our society, a dichotomy is common: one is *either* American *or* foreign, English-speaking *or* Spanish-speaking, Black *or* White. The possibility that one could *at the same time* be Spanish-speaking *and* English-speaking, Vietnamese *and* American, or Black *and* White is hardly considered[3] Yet in Los Angeles, students come from homes that speak more than seventy-seven different languages, including Javenese, Norwegian, Punjabi, Kurdish, and Assyrian.[4] Does this make them "less American" than their counterparts of European descent? The obvious answer to this question is "of course not." The historical answer, too, is a resounding "no." In fact, in 1910, while the number of immigrants entering the United States was smaller, the percentage of our population that was foreign-born was greater, registering at 14.7 percent. In 1990, the foreign-born population was 19.8 million, almost 8 percent of the total population.[5]

The labels that we assign to one another are often inequitable and frequently inaccurate. For instance, by virtue of the label "Hispanic," too often Hispanics are treated as a homogenous group when in actuality they may share little affinity other than the common surnames and the common language of their ancestors. Mexican Americans tend to immigrate for economic reasons, Cuban Americans for political. To treat them as one homogenous group and to collect data as such does a huge disservice to underrepresentation efforts.[6]

Subjective labeling for arbitrary purposes promotes racism, which at its core is an abuse of power. Professor James Horton, of George Washington University, observes, "Virginia law defined a black person as a person with one-sixteenth African ancestry. Florida defined

Students at the World of Opportunity School in Birmingham, Alabama, (a school created to meet the needs of students cast off from public schools) reflect on the powers of labels:

- Labels mean something. When someone labels me . . . I want to knock the cr*p out of them.
- When people call me names . . . I want to fight and curse sometimes.
- Where I used to live and go to school, I felt like I didn't belong because I was always in Special Ed.
- When people call me names, I want to just go and hide.
- When they call me names I just walk away because I know that person doesn't know me at all. So, why should I let petty things bring me down?
- When people put names and titles on me . . . I pray for them.
- When people use labels against me . . . I want to understand their deepest fears of me.

a black person as a person with one-eighth African ancestry. Alabama said, 'You are black if you got any African ancestry at all.' But you know what this means? You can walk across a state line and literally, legally change race. Now, what does race mean under those circumstances? You give me the power, I can make you any race I want you to be, because it is a social, political construction."[7]

The concept of "true Americanism" also seems to permeate geographical boundaries. In a report on underrepresented minority achievement and course taking, researchers Richard Tapia and Cynthia Lanius ask the question, "Have you noticed that as long as teen violence remained confined to cities, it was not seen as an *American* problem, just a big-city one?"[8] They assert that we expect urban minority kids to be violent. In a May 2003 bulletin, the Federal Office of Juvenile Justice and Delinquency Prevention (OJJDP) examined the postulate that the tenets of social disorganization (residential instability, ethnic diversity, female-headed households, and poverty rate) were unique to urban areas. The study found that the principles of

April, an eighteen-year-old GED student, shares her thoughts on violence in her community. Her response reflects the faith articulated by many in her community:

> The reason that I think there is violence in our community is because people stop believing in the Lord. Most people have good heads on their shoulders, but they are hanging with the wrong crowd. I also feel that the parents are not getting involved in their children's lives. Most of these parents are too busy working or staying out late at night.
>
> In order to get our community on the right track, we have to first get right with the Lord. And if parents spend more time with their kids doing positive things, rather than letting them hang out in the streets, there will be less crime in the community and make it a safe place. If we come together as a community and believe in the Lord, we can cut down on the amount of violence. That's not so hard. As I sit outside finishing what I'm writing, I look around and see a lot of young people slamming, banging, and doing drugs. . . . Some people say that their daddy used to do the same thing. I say that you shouldn't want to be like him, you should want to be better than him.

social disorganization theory can be applied to rural communities. In the nonmetropolitan counties that made up the study sample, per capita rates of juvenile arrest for violent offenses were significantly and consistently associated with residential instability, ethnic diversity, and family disruption. Based on the strength and consistency of the findings, family disruption, in particular, appears to be a critical element of social disorganization in nonmetropolitan communities.[9]

In short, then, incidents of violence seem to be more about volume than location. Tapia and Lanius note that when we speak about underrepresented minorities, we are generally referring to the populations in our nation's large cities. In many of the country's major cities, minorities comprise the majority. The districts of Chicago, Houston, Los Angeles, and New York are 85–90 percent underrepresented minori-

Alejandra, a newcomer from Mexico City, is a GED and English-learner student. As part of the two-way road to education at the World of Opportunity School, Alejandra is also the Spanish instructor. She writes in her newly acquired language:

> My principal obstacle in America is learning English because we have to overcome barriers. When you are going places such as the bank, for example, there isn't anybody that speaks Spanish or another foreign language. Our Spanish-speaking people can feel bad—this is their first obstacle and it is frustrating. But all of us have to learn English.

Alejandra also urges her peers to learn English—and she proposes action:

> We can learn by going to schools where English courses are offered. If we look around us, hanging on the walls are signs in different languages, although some people don't make the effort to learn English. After all, the government expended money to make these signs, we should use them to help us learn.
>
> We need to learn English and the best way is going to school. This way we can live together in harmony.

Alejandra also relates her personal goals:

> I want to have friends, learn English, and to know how the other people think. I want to express my ideas so that I can know more about other people and they can know about me more clearly: What do I need? Who am I? What am I doing here? What do I want to be?
>
> In this program where I am studying, there are people here, everyday, to help me to do better.
>
> "Thank you" is not a sufficient word to express how appreciative I feel.

ties.[10] It should be noted, however, that while there are similarities among the factors of social disorganization present in big cities, there are still vast differences among outcomes in urban areas. For example, while San Francisco could boast that 42.3 percent of their students completed courses required for admission to state universities in 1994–1995, only 18.9 percent of students in Oakland accomplished this feat. One reason for the disparities among urban districts is that some have larger concentrations of poor children who may have trouble in school because of lack of resources and guidance at home. In the Los Angeles Unified School District, 70 percent of the students qualify for the federal free-lunch program. In Fresno, 34 percent of children live in extremely impoverished neighborhoods characterized by rampant unemployment, deteriorated buildings, and high crime rates. In Los Angeles, 46.5 percent of the district's students don't speak English well, if at all.[11]

Children and families for whom English is not a primary language are frequently stereotyped in the realm of public perception, and, sadly, sometimes even in the perception of the schools whose aim it is to provide an appropriate education. In a 1998 research project, author Barbara Flores sought to dispel some of the myths concerning students with limited English proficiency. She found that:

- children from diverse backgrounds use language proficiently and bring rich experiences to school.
- using engaging literature, discussing texts and learning in integrated rather than separate settings enriches all children's language and literacy development.
- educators should use a variety of authentic assessment methods to diagnose and plan instruction.
- parents of children of diverse backgrounds are interested in their children's schooling and can be effective educational partners.[12]

Nieto found that the view that poor parents and those who speak another language or come from a dominated culture are unable to provide environments that promote learning can lead to condescending practices that reject the skills and resources they already have.[13]

What, then, are the best practices? Where, then, are the solutions that will lead to greater equity within the diversity of race? First, we must understand that we are already dealing with the proceeds of disparity. Second, we must look at the cycle that creates ongoing inequality, and third, real teaching, infused with multicultural education, must begin.

In speaking about a teacher in Cambridge, Massachusetts, who articulated a desire to not deal with politics, racism, and class exploitation, author Jonathan Kozol holds that the idea—anyone may choose or not choose to be involved in someone else's desperation—depends upon the prior myth that he is not already involved in that desperation's *proceeds*.[14] Indeed, all educators are involved in the proceeds of societal strain. It can be maddening, at times, to absorb the collective stresses of a classroom. While reviewing a book on diversity, a teacher exclaimed, "Many of my colleagues and I have been teaching for at least twenty years. We have adjusted to larger classes, and to more foreign students with minimal English skills. We have learned the names of new rock stars and realize that our young students no longer read for pleasure or know much about the Vietnam War or Jack Kerouac. We have learned to take more excuses for work turned in late or in less proper academic format or language. We empathize with single mothers' hectic lives and with recovering drug addicts' struggles to stay clean. Now several education authors are telling us that we have to change more—that we have to adapt our methods and materials to students' lives and interests more."[15]

In *A White Teacher Talks About Race*, Julie Landsman does not call for new strategies and materials, but rather for a tweaking of the collective conscience of those who currently hold the most power in American society. She says, "I always come back to the necessity for white men and women who are the leaders in this country to recognize the deep-seated inequality in our school system and in our economic structure. It is our job to encourage such recognition by our actions, by our instruction, and by our commitment to change it. Part of this commitment can manifest itself in providing support for students who are trying to avoid the pressure to fail, and in pushing those students who are caught up in such failure to conceive of their lives differently."[16]

Part of dealing with the proceeds of inequality, then, involves breaking the current cycle of power and practice with regard to issues of race. While the solution must involve efforts to equalize material conditions, the real strength of the movement lies in changing long-held attitudes and perceptions. Author Richard Sennet gets to the crux of this issue when he offers, "Radical egalitarians have sometimes argued that if material conditions can be equalized, then mutually respectful behavior will spring forward, 'naturally' and spontaneously. This expectation is psychologically naïve. Even if all unjust inequalities could be removed in society, people would still face the problem of how to shape their worst and their better impulses. Mutuality requires active, expressive work. It must be enacted, performed."[17]

The best means to enact mutuality and address the institutional stress of seemingly never-ending accommodation is through multicultural education. Multicultural education can be controversial because it insists that awareness of issues of social justice and power relations in our society, past and present, are crucially relevant to the future of our society and the priorities and values of the next generation. Multicultural education paves the way for both learning and the preservation of cultural integrity. Schooling for nondominant groups is filled with the tension of accommodation. Mutual accommodation is called for. That is, both teachers and students need to modify their behaviors in the direction of a common goal.[18]

It seems natural that this should happen in a classroom but often it does not. Classrooms are more often trysts of hegemony than clashes of culture. The values and histories of the dominant culture within a classroom seem to permeate with a will of their own. It is not so much an act of commission on the part of the classroom teacher, but an act of the omission of directed cultural bridging. It is sometimes difficult to begin a multicultural dialogue. In *Respect in a World of Inequality*, Richard Sennett comments on this phenomenon. Sennett shares that inequality can breed unease, unease breed a desire to connect, yet the connection itself be of a tacit, silent, reserved sort. This emotional chain of events complicates the precept to "show respect" for someone lower down on the social or economic ladder. People may feel that esteem yet fear to seem condescending, and so hold back. Moreover, awareness of one's own privileges can arouse unease; in modern society people do not speak easily of their superior station in life. Paradoxically, the anxiety of privilege may sharpen awareness of those who have less—an anxiety one would not easily declare.[19]

The first step, then, toward the development of a multicultural classroom is to become a multicultural individual. Inherent in this is involvement in activities that emphasize pluralism. Second, we need to confront our own racism and biases. Third, becoming a multicultural person means learning to see reality from a variety of perspectives.[20] This is not always easy. As I reflect upon my childhood, I am grateful that I had parents who were insightful enough to break the bonds of the stereotypes that they were exposed to as children. When I was five years old, I remember being fascinated with the comedic actor Flip Wilson. I didn't think of him as a forerunner of African American representation in comedy. I wasn't impressed that he had achieved his own prime-time slot in an age when this was a cultural rarity. Instead, I simply knew that he was a man who made me laugh. My parents did nothing to dispel this notion and instead helped me to crayon a message of appreciation to him. I was delighted when I received an autographed picture in return for my efforts. And I was sad when my grandmother came to visit, noted the picture, and turned it face down on my dresser. For the first time, I was made aware that skin color might be important. I remember feeling embarrassed after that, as if the picture could see my grandmother's coarse behavior. My insides hurt for the smiling man inside the frame.

I tell this story not to point fingers but to demonstrate the insidiousness of racism, especially in the less diverse areas of our society. My grandmother grew up in rural Wisconsin, in an area where there are still very few families of other cultures. She judged what she did not understand on the basis of fear and hearsay, the natural parents of intolerance. Fear of the unknown is certainly not unique to my grandmother's generation. Only a few short years ago, when I was the principal of a thriving middle school located only a few short hours from several diverse, highly populated urban areas, I was distraught to hear a parent share her concern that her adolescent daughters would not swim in a hotel pool because they were afraid of their African American peers. Author Julie Landsman speaks of a time when her African American housekeeper remonstrated her, at age four, for using the word "nigger" in a children's rhyme. Her housekeeper shared that the word hurt her feelings. Landsman's reaction contains the necessity for ongoing dialogues in our schools and our homes about issues of race.

> This was a time when my body registered pain all through the pathways to my heart. It felt worse than anything I had felt before, to be told that I hurt someone. I believe now that it is in these moments—in the education that we receive that has nothing to do with school—that we are formed. In the heat of our kitchens, in the back of a car, in the check-out lines in stores: this is where our learning takes place. Here is where our impulses are born, our instincts created. And we bring all this into our classrooms, our boardrooms, and meeting places.[21]

In *The Night is Dark and I am Far from Home,* Jonathan Kozol supports this notion of "incidental teaching." Kozol comments that in the classroom, lifestyle is at the heart of education. The things a teacher does not dare to say may well provide a deeper, more substantial, and more lasting lesson than the content of the textbooks or the conscious message of the posters on the wall. The teacher who does not speak to grief, who cannot cry for shame, who does not laugh and will not weep, teaches many deep and memorable lessons about tears, laughter, grief, *and* shame. What the teacher "teaches" is by no means chiefly in the words he speaks. It is at least in part in what he *is*, in what he *does*, and in what he seems to *wish to be*.[22]

If a classroom teacher wishes to be fully effective, she must not let her students be culturally deprived. That is, she must not let the richness of the ethnic landscape be glossed over. Any student who emerges into our culturally diverse society speaking only one language and with a monocultural perspective on the world can legitimately be considered educationally ill prepared. Corporate America wants not people whose heads are stuffed with soon-to-be-obsolete information, but rather people who know how to get access to information, who can critically interpret this information to discover what is relevant and useful, and who can work cooperatively across cultural, linguistic, and racial boundaries.[23]

In order to embrace multiculturalism, we must move beyond the concept of tolerance. When we speak of tolerance in today's public schools, too often it is in the context of "zero tolerance." Zero tolerance is, of course, those behaviors that we will absolutely not put up with. Tolerance, then, is immediately bathed in a negative light. When we later ask students to practice tolerance, we are really asking them only to bear the presence or the actions of others. This falls far short of effecting real and lasting change.

Nonetheless, teaching tolerance should not be discounted because tolerance is really at the root of all growth. What we will eventually accept, we must first be able to bear. Simple endurance, however, will not cause the perceptual shift necessary to create change. My parents have always had an avid interest in antiques, and more often than not, I was made to haunt antique stores with them on their frequent weekend excursions. I didn't usually welcome their jaunts into the dry and dusty world of the past, but it was during such a foray that a lifetime perceptual shift occurred for me. I was idly leafing through a series of old photographs, marking the time until my parents had finished with their own searching, when I was stopped short. There in front of me was a picture of Jesus and his lambs. It was quite similar to the picture that to this day hangs above my bed, save for one important difference. The figure of Jesus in the picture that I held that day in the antique shop was not the Caucasian Jesus of my Sunday school books, but was instead a regal African American Jesus. I was at first flabbergasted and then excited, and I rushed to show my mother the picture and to share with her the cognitive shift that had been inspired within me. Her reaction was an important part of the process of perceptual shift. "How wonderful," she said, "and how lucky we all are that there is room for so many different cultures in our world. What a neat thing for you to discover!" When I think of the moments like these, in which our value systems are altered, I am awed by the power of adult influence in a child's life. As adults, we are provided a sacred trust that we will not close minds but will, instead, leave them open to the levels of acceptance and respect that can be directed from the gateways of tolerance.

Nieto uses these same constructs in her efforts on behalf of the diversity movement. Beyond tolerance, there is a variety of levels of support for pluralism: acceptance, respect, affirmation, solidarity, and critique. Acceptance is the second level of support for diversity. If we accept differences we at the very least acknowledge them without denying their importance. Respect is the third level of multicultural education. Respect means to admire and hold in high esteem. Affirmation, solidarity, and critique are based on the premise that the most powerful learning results when students work and struggle with one another, even if that work is sometimes difficult and challenging.[24]

In my own classroom, where there is only minimal cultural diversity, there is an ongoing discussion of dignity. I try to teach the students not only about the traits of character but also about how words of disrespect, intolerance of another's habits, or dismissal of another's values are affronts to dignity. For the most part, the students are gentle with one another. Those that I teach are educationally disadvantaged because they are nontraditional learners. They understand, firsthand, the fragility of the human spirit and the impact of judgment upon drive. On a subconscious level, they realize that the traits of acceptance, respect, and dignity are not only the answers to inequities of race, but are also the answers to a whole spectrum of injustices. They confide their dreams in whispers and wait to see if they will be affirmed or shattered. They realize their own power as they hear others do the same. They hold their breath and cautiously wait for the proverbial other shoe to fall . . . and when it does not, they learn to breathe together. Laugh together. Grow together. Resiliency has its roots in tolerance and its blossoms in respect. It is vital that we teach today's children to sow the seeds of a better tomorrow.

Please Sir, I Want Some More

The face of poverty is the face of a child. The faces of thousands of children who sit in tidy rows in classrooms each day. They sit in threadbare clothing with stomachs that rumble from hunger. They have not had breakfast and they will not have supper. They will have only the school's federally subsidized food that day. It is 8 o'clock and they are looking forward to lunchtime. They learn to dread weekends because the possibility of one adequate meal may rely on patience or a pocketbook.

The face of poverty is the face of an adolescent. Working cooperatively in a classroom with one eye on the clock. Soon it will be time to ditch the last class of the day and head to a restaurant where there are a thousand remnants of food left on delicate china to be scraped away before the plates are washed. Their parents have told them that if they work hard, they can get ahead. And maybe it is true, because they've always had enough to eat. They notice, though, that the patrons of the restaurant do not exist on macaroni and cheese and cheap cereal. They scrape steak into a large disposal that whirs and crunches with regularity, and they wait for the American dream.

The face of poverty is the face of a teen. Classrooms filled with teens with sad, knowing eyes and the perpetual defensive shrugs

In *Amazing Grace,* Jonathan Kozol shares a glimpse into life in the South Bronx:

These rats are fearless. Light don't scare them. Noise don't scare them. You can see them in the park at noon." She tells me of a seven-month-old boy who was attacked by several rats who had climbed into his crib. "Doctor said he hadn't seen bite marks like that in years. The baby's fingers were all bloody. I think it was the third time that this baby was attacked. His mother's terrified but can't move out. The city put her in this building and she don't have any money to move somewhere else.[25]

meant to communicate that they just don't care. Teens who would like to go to the prom yet feel trapped by the street. Teens who are called irresponsible in the classroom because homework was neglected in the name of surrogate parenting. Teens who are smart enough to go to college, who yearn to better themselves, but who, even with scholarships, will have nothing to pack in their suitcase, no way to fit in, and thus, no way to thrive. Another heavy minute encased in four walls that feel like a holding pen. Another shrug. Another reason to wonder if the struggle is worth the diploma.

In his inaugural address, President John F. Kennedy let the word go forth about the domestic as well as the foreign policy attitude of his administration, declaring, "If the free society cannot help the many who are poor, it cannot save the few who are rich."[26] Much has been written about poverty. A search of the Web produces several alleged antidotes to poverty. Prescriptions like marriage, higher education, work, and increased economic development are all offered as panaceas to being poor. Education is mentioned frequently as a cure for economic disadvantage. Federally mandated programs, such as Head Start (instituted during the Johnson administration), have attempted to address the connection between education and economic sufficiency for a number of years. Head Start, for the Johnsons, was a "family

Students at the World of Opportunity School speak of how their school has helped them overcome feelings of defeat:

- Since going back to get my GED, I am not ashamed of asking for help when it comes down to a simple problem. Sometimes, I get frustrated but it doesn't make me give up, because once I get my GED, I can work in a hospital facility office, filing medical records, or taking care of patients in nursing homes.

- My children come first because they look up to me. And I look up to getting my GED, and learning the new things that I have never learned before in Certified Nurses Aide (CNA) class.

- I've found the WOO to be a very good school for someone who is "real" about school. Coming here has affected my morals as a young man to try even harder to reach my many goals.

- The WOO has affected my life by helping me not give up, by helping me keep a positive attitude, by encouraging me to reach out to my peers and make friends, and by helping me to come to class and staying as long as possible.

- I help my cousin when she needs help with her work. The WOO has affected my life by knowing I have the knowledge and ability to help her.

- The way I think now is good. I'm a better man in the things that I do.

- I think very differently now because I know in order to be what I want to be in life this study is a must. I want to make myself and my Mom proud.

- One thing I've done at the WOO that makes me feel the most proud is coming here everyday. There isn't anybody trying to start problems. I'm trying to get my GED peacefully. And, I'm looking to get a good job.

- I'm here getting my education because I have two kids and one on the way. I don't want to find myself in a position where my kids are coming to me, asking me to help them with their homework and I can't because I never had an education. That's why I'm here today to learn something and that's what I'm proud of. I'm learning something for my kids.

affair. It was a bit like working on the family farm," said Luci Johnson. "Instead of raising corn and alfalfa, we raised hopes and opportunities. My father thought that the passport out of poverty was education. If you started school on an uneven plane, it was like starting a race with your shoelaces tied together. If you had your physical, emotional, and psychological distractions resolved, you could take advantage of those educational opportunities afforded to you. If not, you would be defeated before you ever began."[27]

Current educational theorists argue that while education may, indeed, be a passport toward financial stability, it is not an antidote to poverty. In *Education and Justice,* Edmund Gordon writes,

> Education is not an antidote to poverty. Furthermore, the school is immoral when it continues to hold that as its goal. Education is concerned with the total development of people and their preparation for the multiple roles that make up their lives. Schools are one of the resources by which society prepares and develops its members. When other societal resources are unequally distributed, quality of schooling becomes even more important. When the society produces subpopulations less well prepared to benefit from the standard offerings of the school, we have the additional responsibility for broadening, expanding and enriching the offerings of our schools, not as our first line of defense against poverty, but as protection against the effects of an unjust society, which if they go uncorrected, systematically erode the human resources of that society.[28]

This same thought is voiced by civic leaders across the United States. That's because the real antidote to poverty is something money can't buy; it's an attitude shift at a fundamental level and on a grand scale.

"People have a strong tendency to look at the world in terms of 'them and us,'" says Norm Monroe, staff assistant to Beverly Stein, chair of the Multnomah County Board of Commissioners in Portland, Oregon. "We isolate [the poor] in all ways, and we foster their dysfunction by treating them poorly. We see that play out in our value systems: we say we're well, they're sick. We see in it our

Students describe the lunchrooms and bathrooms at their inner-city schools:

> The bathroom was a smoke break for as long as a teacher don't come in. The lunchroom was the skipping spot and there were food fights. The lunchroom was not clean. There were rats everywhere and the room was always dirty.

> There was always grease on the dishes and on the dining room floor.

WOO poet Ebony writes:

> Every time you go in the bathroom
> you always see pads on the floor.
> Every time you go to use the restroom,
> you go in believing you will turn right back around.
> Every time you try and wash your hands
> the sink's always overflowing.
> And when they try to keep it clean
> you always have some nut-ball messing it back up.
> They need to keep the restroom clean.
> They need to keep soap in the restroom.
> They need to keep the floors mopped and waxed.
> They need to keep the trash off the floor.
> They need to keep all of the kids who are skipping
> out of the restroom.

public-policy planning: we tend to plan for and around poor people but not *with* them."[29]

Are we planning with the poor when we educate them in portable classrooms? Or worse, when we cram them into rooms that once housed day-care centers, music programs, and computer labs? What about when we try to promote learning in teachers' lounges, auditoriums, and in the corners of libraries that once held books? Class-size reduction has been touted as a best practice for academic remediation and it is proven that having smaller number of students in classes can increase learning. However, for some teachers and policy makers, the struggle by urban schools to take advantage of the class-size reduction program raises the issue of equity. They question whether it is a good idea for the policy to be uniformly applied across diverse districts. "The schools that don't have room for class-size reduction are often the ones serving minorities and disadvantaged children, who perhaps would benefit from smaller classes the most," says Barbara Miller, the research director at EdSource, a Palo Alto research organization. "It's an irony no one can escape."[30]

Edmund Gordon details another irony of the poor. He shares that for society at large, quality of schooling is a relatively unimportant correlate of achievement; yet for poor and minority children, quality of schooling—teacher characteristics, kinds of materials available, amount of teacher training, money spent on schooling—is more strongly associated with achievement. When support for academic learning is not a part of the natural environment, the relatively modest support supplied by the school did make a difference.[31] Unfortunately, levels of even modest support are declining. Under the tentacles of the No Child Left Behind Act, support is seen as synonymous with reformation. But some reforms, particularly those focusing on "raising standards," such as longer school days and fewer "frills" such as music and art, have been felt most profoundly at schools serving poor and culturally subordinated students.[32] Simply put, standards do not alter equity. It is not equitable that our nation's poor should not sing or draw or have recess. It is inappropriate to threaten a child who shivers with cold, whose last meal was two days ago, or who does not have a home to return to at the end of the day. It is irresponsible to ask a child to bypass his own milestones in order to keep up with his more advantaged peers. It is a governmental mockery to say that no child will be left behind as we plod along in a system that leaves every child behind. Consider the words of Julie Landsman:

When I think of the times I have lost all hope, of the times I have been clinically depressed, I know I could not imagine relief from pain—not the next day and not the next week. If any of our students feel this, for whatever reason, we have failed them. If they do not come to school, every one of them, with a sense of hope and celebration, each and every day when they arrive in our classrooms, we are failing them. We are failing all of them: the white boys in their thin sweaters and bare feet in mid-January, the black girls in veils and head coverings, the cheerleaders with their stick-thin bodies and their large, mascara'ed eyes.[33]

And then consider the timeless words of Jonathan Kozol:

Children go to school to learn how *not* to interrupt the evil patterns that they see before then, how *not* to question and how *not* to doubt: to learn to vote with reasonable regularity, to kill on orders, and to sleep eight hours without grief. They go to school to learn to be proficient at mechanical procedures, docile in the absence of all processes they do not understand, acquiescent in the presence of a seeming barbarism. It is not so much that they learn to be "cruel" people. Rather it is, they learn that it is not needful to be urgent in compassion or importunate in justice. Not positive desolation, but a genial capability for well-behaved abstention in the presence of despair: this is the innocence we teach our children.[34]

A Capital Curriculum

On the day that school pictures were taken, all of my seventh-grade students shuffled through the line, clutching their payment envelopes and combing their hair. Andres stood in line, too, with no envelope in his hands. I asked him, quietly, if he'd forgotten it and he shook his head. "We're not getting pictures," he explained, "this is just for the yearbook." He didn't seem to care whether his hair was smoothed or his collar straightened. He stood in the line looking bored and impatient. When he approached the desk, he mumbled his name, telling the photographer's assistant that he did not want to purchase pictures.

A few weeks later, the pictures arrived. Being typical students, my students first frowned at their pictures and then glowed as they showed them to their friends. Across my classroom, someone shouted to Andres, "Hey, where are your pictures?"

I answered for Andres. "Some people get their pictures taken elsewhere and don't get school pictures."

But Andres was quick to interject. "Not me." His voice carried through my small classroom. "My family is too poor for pictures. I don't get them taken anywhere. Ever." Silence descended on my classroom until another student suggested that we get the digital camera and retake everyone's picture. She said that a digital picture would be just as good. Andres smiled and with his usual diplomacy suggested that everyone give him one of their pictures. Soon, the scissors were flying and pictures were being exchanged and the heaviness of the moment faded from their adolescent minds.

We are told that we live in the richest country in the world. And it is true that resource capital is in good supply in the United States. But there are critical problems in the distribution of these resources and in access to most low-status people. In the absence of access to essential human resource capital, there may well be limits to what any within-school educational reform can achieve.[35] School pictures, of course, are not critical to the curriculum of a child. They are, instead, a by-product of the resource of financial capital. Monies for field trips, sports, and schoolwide donations for the needy also rely on financial capital.

There are other forms of capital, too, that must be present in adequate measure before learning can take place. Health capital, human capital (social competence), and social capital (networking and values) all play a role in the development of healthy affects and intellects. Indeed, it seems that the loftiest aim of a public education should be the development of personal capital. That is, possessing a disposition, attitudes, and aspirations that lead to a sense of personal empowerment.

The nemesis of the development of personal capital is a lockstep, top-down, one-size-fits-all curricular model. Forcing children to walk along the same path does not force them to also walk a mile in one

Consider the strength behind this older GED student's words and experiences:

My name is LaWanda and this is my story:

When I was young I really don't remember having much and I mean much of anything . . . no clothes, food, and as a matter of fact, not too many of the basic necessities I needed to make it on an everyday cycle, but I made it. You see my mother was a smart beautiful lady but she had a serious drug problem. This went on for most of my grade school years and all of my teenage years.

When I started high school I didn't have the things like the other girls had and I was very depressed during this time because I wanted to fit in and I couldn't. I was teased a lot about how I looked, my clothes, shoes, etc. You see that bothered me but I got used to it.

School name-calling bothered me a lot, but it was when I got home and was called names that it really hurt. You see, even though my mom had a drug problem, she was very good at putting people down and making you feel like you were nothing but a problem she had to be bothered with.

Because my self-esteem was so low, I dropped out of school and ran to the arms of a man that I thought was the best thing ever—only to be let down again. He considered me nothing. He called me things: "stupid, sorry, ugly, good for nothing." He even called me "b__ __ __ h" and "wh __ __ e" (and the sad thing was that we had two children). This caused me to think that I was less than nothing. Living with this man, my home life, and my mom made me angry and everything I did, I did out of anger. I got on drugs and started to dance and sell my body because I felt like that's all I could do, like that's all I was good enough for. I wanted to kill them both!

But now I realize that I am somebody, and that I can have a nice, healthy, and safe life for myself and my kids. You see, God has blessed me with some new names like: blessed woman of god, and the one I am most proud of is Mom. You need to know that these days people, family, institutions, can not label me. I learned the hard way that I don't need no one to validate who I am. (emphasis added) another's shoes. Instead, we teach some to stride and some to stumble. In *Dumbing Us Down*, John Gatto noted,

> I've noticed a fascinating phenomenon in my twenty-five years of teaching: that schools and schooling are increasingly irrelevant to the great enterprises of the planet. No one believes anymore that scientists are trained in science classes or politicians in civics classes. The truth is that schools don't really teach anything except how to obey orders. . . . Although teachers do care and work very, very hard, the institution is psychopathic; it has no conscience. It rings a bell and the young man in the middle of writing a poem must close his notebook and move to a different cell where he must memorize that humans and monkeys derive from a common ancestor. . . . It is absurd and anti-life to be part of a system that compels you to sit in confinement with people of exactly the same age and social class. That system effectively cuts you off from the immense diversity of life and the synergy of variety; indeed, it cuts you off from your own past and future, sealing you in a continuous present much the same way television does.[36]

It would be naïve to assert that developing personal capital alone is a redress of poverty. Poverty can not be answered solely by the teacher or only by reduced-rate student lunches, nor by the provision of school materials for those with great need. Poverty is not answered by fee-free sports programs, the waiver of school fees, or by breakfast programs and affordable after-school care programs. The poverty faced by over two million Americans, 18 percent of whom are children, does not have a single cure; however, it is the duty of all who work with children to soothe and to smooth wherever possible. A warm coat soothes a cold child. A hot breakfast and a balanced lunch smooth the jagged edges of hunger. Participation in sports and other cocurricular options may soothe a restless youth and may keep him from the streets, just as an after-school program may be doing for his younger sister.

When author Jonathan Kozol addresses audiences on the issues associated with educational inequity, he satirizes some of his affluent colleagues who ask him, in all seriousness, whether money is really the answer to poverty. Money, Kozol asserts, is certainly one answer

In *The Night is Dark and I am Far from Home*, Kozol relates a friend's longing for a coat:

"How I like to go into a real store down there on Newbury Street and put down forty dollars and bring home a new coat for me to wear. A brand new coat for me to wear. A brand new coat: pay forty dollars. Buy it new, and bring it home that day; not buy it on time-payment." It's not that difficult for me to get ahold of the cash. The next day, I put it in an envelope with a brief note, embarrassed. I go to visit a month later. She says, "Sylvia, come on out, let Jonathan see you in your new coat." She says: "No, wait. I'll tell you just what happened if you promise not to get mad. I went downtown to all the nice stores. It was just about two weeks ahead of Christmas, so I took the children with me. They don't say nothing; but I keep on seeing Sylvia look back into the windows of the stores. She don't say nothing but I see her keep on looking. I see that look and I know she be wanting something nice and pretty for her to wear to school, but she want me to have mine first. She be so good, Jonathan, I near to cry. She didn't want me to give up the coat I planned on for so long. . . ." She stops; then she calls out once more into the back room: "Sylvia, you come right in, let me and Jonathan see you in your new coat. . . ."[37]

to poverty and is many times the best and most capable equalizer. Kozol speaks from the heart and in his writings, too, he often shares the stories of his friends who reside in the poverty-stricken neighborhoods where he spends his time.

The stories of the poor must be told because consciousness must be raised. Awareness and empathy building are more vital to a classroom than an academic curriculum. If we remove from classrooms the ability to actively teach the foundations of character because we are myopically focused on test scores and headlines, then issues of poverty will always be issues of too little and too late. Educational justice can not be delivered if disadvantaged individuals are made to play "catch up" with regard to personal or financial capital. When this is the case, the rest of the world is inevitably one step ahead.

The village that houses the poor has the greatest stake in the eradication of poverty. In 1998, three Chicago police officers strove to provide their community with a model to follow for community reformation. In their book, *The Slick Boys*, the officers outlined a ten-point plan for community involvement.

1. Serve and protect your brothers and sisters—remember that we are all related as human beings.
2. Speak the language—become part of a culture instead of being on the outside looking in. Ask questions. Become involved. Care.
3. Be a ray of hope—people naturally turn toward hope.
4. Don't play to stereotypes—write your own life scripts. Base your beliefs on what's real and not on hearsay.
5. Give something back.
6. Education is key.
7. Have big expectations—don't let low expectations become a self-fulfilling prophecy.
8. Respect one another.
9. Lead by example.
10. Help people one by one, one *to* one.[38]

Mind Discrimination

There is an old parable about Felix the frog and his human companion, Clarence. One day, in an effort to achieve fame, fortune, and the rest of the American dream, Clarence decided that he would teach Felix to fly. A flying frog was sure to reap great rewards! Clarence read books, gained knowledge about motivation and behavior, and commenced to work with poor Felix rigorously. After his fall from the window of the first story, Felix was bumped and bruised. At the second story, he was crying and pleading. "Please, Clarence," he said. "Frogs are not meant to fly!" But Clarence simply ignored him. And at the third story, Felix was silent and resigned. Eventually, of course, Felix ceased to be. And what was Clarence's reaction to the demise of his protégé? Clarence, it is said, announced, "Next time, I'll get a smarter frog!"

Clarence's problem, of course, is not only that he set out to do the improbable but also that he used only one tactic to attempt to get results. Had his mind been more open, perhaps he could have seen that a bit of the Wright brothers' flair might have better accomplished his goal. Perhaps, too, he might have realized that a talking frog was already pretty unique. Had Clarence focused less on a strict adherence to methodology and more on the needs of his learner, Felix might still be alive and Clarence might have been a very rich man.

Several years ago, Apple Computer paid tribute to those men and women who are or were in their time considered divergent thinkers. "Think Different" was the message that accompanied posters of history makers such as Albert Einstein, Jackie Robinson, Martha Graham, and Pablo Picasso. Apple included this poem with their literature:

Here's to the Crazy Ones

Here's to the crazy ones.
  The misfits.
  The rebels.
    The troublemakers.
    The round pegs in the square holes.
    The ones who see things differently.

        They're not fond of rules.
    And they have no respect for the status quo.

    You can praise them, disagree with them, quote them,
        disbelieve them, glorify or vilify them.
  About the only thing you can't do is ignore them.
    Because they change things.

They invent.   They imagine.   They heal.
They explore.   They create.   They inspire.
They push the human race forward.
Maybe they have to be crazy.

How else can you stare at an empty canvas and see a work of art?
Or sit in silence and hear a song that's never been written?
Or gaze at a red planet and see a laboratory on wheels?

We make tools for these kinds of people.

While some see them as the crazy ones,
we see genius.

Because the people who are crazy enough to think
they can change the world, are the ones who do.[39]

I have a police officer friend who confesses that his high school teachers did not expect him to graduate. He says that they feared not only for his academics but also for his personal safety. I know of a master hairdresser who travels the country, motivationally speaking while showing off the latest techniques with hair, who dropped out of high school and later achieved his GED. He is warm and whimsical and believes in the power of positive thinking, affirming others, and building hope. He says that school provided the most miserable twelve years of his life. I know of a car mechanic mogul who has built an empire on the foundation of providing quality service in an atmosphere that feels emotionally safe for car owners. He related to a group of educators who were touring one of his facilities that he hated school and that he was the worst nightmare of all of his teachers.

What do each of these men have in common, in addition to an intense dislike of institutionalized education? Each of them embodies the characteristics of a divergent thinker with attention-span issues that interfered with a traditional teaching styles. Author Thom Hartmann writes of "Farmers and Hunters." Farmers tend to be focused individuals who have good attention to detail, work well with others, are not easily bored, and who view patience and a slow and steady progression toward a goal as desirable traits. Farmers are most amenable to traditional classroom methodologies. Hunters, on the other hand, are intuitive, flexible, visual thinkers for whom time is elastic. They are able to throw themselves fully into each hunt with incredible bursts of energy, and they are adept at changing strategies on a moment's notice. They are easily bored and view risk-taking as a desirable facet of life. In classrooms, Hunters tend to be labeled attention deficit hyperactivity disordered (ADHD) and often experience a great deal of difficulty with traditional curriculum.[40]

Hartmann goes on to assert that our schools are set up along Farmer lines. Sit quietly at the desk, children are told, while the teacher talks and points to pages in the book. Ignore the child next to you who is sniffling; don't rattle your papers; don't look ahead in

Children's author Dav Pilkey is probably best known for his "Captain Underpants" series of books. In two of his "About the Author" bios, Dav shared the following,

When Dav Pilkey was a kid, his teachers thought he was disruptive, "behaviorally challenged," and in serious need of a major attitude adjustment. When he wasn't writing sentences in the detention room, he could usually be found sitting at his private desk out in the hallway. There he spent his time writing and drawing his own original comic books about a superhero named Captain Underpants.[41]

When Dav Pilkey was in elementary school, he was always getting into trouble for pulling pranks, cracking jokes, and making silly comic books. In second grade, he invented his most famous (or infamous) character, CAPTAIN UNDERPANTS! Dav's teacher told him, "You'd better straighten up, young man, because you can't spend the rest of your life making silly books." Dav was not a very good listener![42]

the book. To a smart Hunter with a low boredom threshold, this is torture! It's a prescription for failure.

My book *Uphill Both Ways: Helping Students Who Struggle in School*,[43] is dedicated to outlining strategies for better inclusion of all learners. A strong case is made for a constructivist curriculum, for the infusion of character education, and for education steeped in the multiple intelligences. I've included the learners who struggle in school in a chapter on diversity, too, because they are discriminated against by classroom teachers on a daily basis. Often, when students cross over the educational equator that exists between the third and fourth grades, teachers expect them to abandon their Hunter behaviors. Students with little concept of time are expected to get homework done on time. Daydreaming is not seen as the incubation period for bursts of creativity; rather it is categorized as rudeness or apathy. It is taken for granted in an adult society that we cannot all be generalists skilled in every area of learning and mastery. Nevertheless, we apply tremendous pressure on our children to be good at *everything*. Every day they are expected to shine in math, reading, writing, speaking, spelling, memorization, comprehension, problem solving, socialization, athletics, and following verbal directions. Few, if any, children can master all of these "trades." And none of us adults can. In one way or another, all minds have their specialties and their frailties. Some price, modest or substantial, must be paid any time a mind is forced or attempts to learn or perform something in a way for which it is not wired. This happens to all of us from time to time, but the outcome is tragic when the mismatching of a mind to a set of important tasks becomes a daily event and when that poor fit is not understood. This phenomenon takes place every day in schools everywhere.[44]

Author Thomas Armstrong speaks to four common classroom practices that encourage discrimination toward diverse learners. He calls them the "Four Ts That Kill Learning": Talk, Textbooks, Task Analysis, and Tracking. One-fifth of teaching is "frontal teaching" that elicits no response or exchange from an audience of learners. This

Carole Anne, GED student and an arts and crafts/jewelry instructor at the WOO, displays her determination in spite of her earlier school experiences:

> When I was still in school my teacher had her own way of picking on me. She would say, "Carole Anne, read this page," knowing very well that my so-called "friends" would laugh at me. She wouldn't do anything when she would hear someone say, "LD Freak," or "look at her, she's Learning Dumb."
>
> Everyday it happened. I never told my mother, but somehow she knew and put me in two different schools in one year.
>
> Finally, I told my mother, "I'm not going to be picked on anymore. I'm not going to make you hear the teacher say at an IEP anymore, "She may never learn to spell or read."
>
> I got angry. I started reading one book a month until by the next school year, at the age of 16, instead of reading at a 3rd grade level, I was reading at an 8th grade level. And, now I'm in GED classes and don't hear, "You'll never finish."
>
> I say to myself, "I'm going to do it! I WILL get my GED, and I will try hard to get into Fashion School."

means that some learners may tune out 20 percent of information, specifically that information that is important enough for the teacher to emphasize during lecture. Textbooks, too, resist interaction in a very literal sense—students are not allowed to write in them and must turn them in at the end of the year. Task analysis can result in a fragmented approach to learning for wholistic learners. The bedrock of this form of educational malpractice is those fill-in-the-blank worksheets meant to teach an isolated skill such as learning the "ph" sound. Finally, given that the theory of multiple intelligences asserts that intellect is reflected through at least eight different ways of thinking, tracking students based upon their abilities in only one or two intelligence areas harms those students who are in lower groups.[45]

In addressing these issues, author Sonia Nieto shared the following:

When this happens on a school-wide or university-wide level, it is institutional racism of the most insidious kind. We who are raised to speak quietly, to face our teachers directly, or to work on our own assume that the way we learned is the best way for all kids to learn. Because we are comfortable with learning in silence and solitude, we assume are students are comfortable like this. Because we have been encouraged to think of ourselves first and our community or even our family, second, we assume the same values on the part of the kids we teach.[46]

My son's karate instructor is the most natural teacher that I have ever had the opportunity to observe. It is clear that he loves the martial arts. He is adept at pacing for all levels of learners, has a consistently positive mental attitude, and high expectations for his students. On a few occasions, he has shared that a traditional approach to education was difficult for his kinesthetic learning style. His joy and his expertise in the martial arts demonstrate that there is a niche in which every individual can excel. My son's karate instructor does not have a four-year teaching degree; he has something more valuable. He has power and an ability to use that power to evoke respect and create positive self-images for his pupils.

The best antidote to educational injustice in the area of diversity is to hone the values of respect in our students. *They watch us all the time.* The students, that is. They listen to us, sometimes. They learn from all that watching and listening. Be quiet. Don't cheat. Pick up. Don't lie. Be nice. Don't fight. They attend to us, more than we usually realize. We yell to get the cafeteria quiet—a delicious irony, not lost on them—and we whisper to a child who is embarrassed to talk. We assign books that we have not read carefully and waste our students' time, or else together we discover a new and exciting resource.[47]

One resolution to inequality requires a shift in power and a shift in the way that power is used. My son's karate teacher—former student rebel, nonconformist, and nontraditional learner—ends each of his classes by having the students say the credo, "Might for Right." May we all consider this each day in our classrooms.

CHAPTER TWO

Inequity Within Assessment

All bad precedents begin as justifiable measures.
—Julius Caesar[1]

Belay On

Have you ever noticed that time rarely carries us back to places of childhood achievement? When a coworker asks me to spell a word for them, for example, and it rolls off my tongue with ease, I am not taken back in time to spelling bees that I won or even to spelling tests that I aced. Why is it, then, that times of inadequacy seem to haunt us, even twenty-five years after they have occurred?

I am picturing being ten years old and in gym class. We are taking that test, the one in which the president honors those among us who are fit, and I am gazing at the long rope that is anchored securely, I hope, to the ceiling far above. I know without a doubt that I will not be able to climb that rope. For three years now, I have slunk to the back of the line, grasped at the rope when I could no longer avoid my turn, and then I hung there, like a fish on a hook. I wait for my arms to move and I will my legs to do something besides embrace the scratchy fibers of the rope. It never happens, though, and soon, I let go of the rope, plop to the ground, and understand that the president, once again, will not be hearing about me.

Time flashes forward . . . far forward . . . and I am standing next to my son in karate class, wondering what I have done. It is a family class and I wanted to show my support for him. He has been in karate over a year and is very good at it. At seven, he has a finesse and a physical savvy that I have never had. We learn to kick and to punch. We learn forms and routines. And my stomach hurts. My punches at the air are dainty, my long fingernails attesting to the fact that I'm more at home in a salon than a gym. My kicks are soft. I want to be anywhere else. As I look around the class, I am amazed that others are relaxed and having fun. It comes time for an individual demonstration and my mouth is dry and my palms are sweaty. I wonder at this oxymoron, preferring to think about the biology of such a phenomenon rather than at the impending doom of public performance. I am ten years old and standing at the rope again. My turn comes and my performance is perfunctory and unimpressive, at best. My face is red. My eyes downcast. I have written books. Spoken to hundreds of people across the nation. Yet it is not until that simple karate form is over and the instructor has moved on that I truly feel brave. It has taken more courage to do what I believe that I am not good at than to do a hundred of the activities at which I excel.

My son is thirteen years old now and a second-degree black belt. Family class, thankfully, was removed from the karate class schedule and I opted not to pursue karate further. I look at my orange belt, sometimes, though, and remind myself what sheer will can do. I was at work the other day and received an email from my son, who had a day off from school. "I'm board." It said. I wrote back to him, suggesting that he work on some homework. His response was immediate. "I'm board. Not despret." I laughed aloud and then despaired. A seventh grader who still spells phonetically. Would the world be a kind place for him? I knew that for him, spelling was like that dangling rope. That he used to get a stomachache on spelling test days. That learning even most of the words required short-term memory tricks. That seeing others excel with ease made him feel inadequate. I still don't know if my active knowledge of his struggles can mitigate them enough. Sometimes, I have moments of flash-forward. Will he someday be poised, pen in hand, needing to write a communication to a colleague and will his palms begin to sweat? Will the tools of character and self-concept that he'd received as a child be enough to make him brave?

It was significant to me, in my ten-year-old mind, that I was somehow disappointing the president with my lack of coordination. Just as it was significant to my son, when he came home bearing the Presidential Physical Fitness Award in his hand, that he was impressing the president. Children do not understand assessment in the way that adults do. The world of a child is often very black and white. One is either athletic or one is not. One is smart or one is not. One is a good speller or one is not. The feedback that we are given in our youth can have dramatic effects on the people that we grow to be.

Assessment is among the most maligned words in public education. Over the course of time, it has been badly battered by the swinging of the education pendulum. Time and time again, politicians and policymakers have returned to the notion that standardized tests offer an appropriate system of checks and balances within public education. The 1970s, for instance, saw an eruption of interest in "minimum competency testing." Reformers sought to improve education by holding educators and students accountable for achieving standards of performance, using tests for high school graduation and/or grade-to-grade promotion. By the 1980s nearly 75 percent of states had some form of minimum competency testing requirements.[2] It was *A Nation at Risk*[3] that truly propelled high stakes into the testing arena. No longer was it enough to profess minimum competency—there must be a higher bar for the greater good. After all, businesses were failing. It couldn't be due to a nationally recognized economic slump. It could not be due to the emergence of vast technology onto a previously manual marketplace. It could not even be due to managerial incompetence. No, instead, the reason for the risk had to lie in the children and the schools. The pressure to force children and teachers into a new mold began and was sealed tight by the mandates imposed by the No Child Left Behind Act.

The notion of assessment, that is, the idea that learning must be evaluated in order for progress to occur, is rooted in good educational practice. The word *assessment* comes from the Latin word *asidere*, which means "to sit beside." In its purest form, assessment is *for* learning not *of* learning. But the pendulum will not stop to discern the good from the bad, and appropriate evaluation is paired with high stakes and standardized practice.

In an analysis of the legal implications of high-stakes assessment, S. E. Phillips of Michigan State University listed these characteristics of high-stakes assessment:

- Public scrutiny of individuality and identifiable results
- A significant gain in money, property, or prestige for those with positive assessment results
- A considerable pressure on individuals or institutions to perform well or raise scores
- A perception that significant individual decisions are being made based on a single imperfect piece of data over which the affected entity has little or no input or control
- Complex and costly security procedures designed to ensure maximum fairness for all who are assessed.[4]

By its own definition, high-stakes assessment is dangerous. Randy Hoover and Kathy L. Shook of Youngstown State University express a concern for those most harshly affected by the arbitrary sanctions and climate of current school reform. Hoover and Shook state, "Educators are deskilled and held to arbitrary outcomes that have little or nothing to do with what happens in schools. They are denied professional decision making latitude in working with their pupils as they know they can best serve them. Schoolchildren are, likewise, visible victims of sorting by socioeconomic status and being classified arbitrarily by high stakes tests that fail to meet recognized scientific standards of test validity and violate all learned society guidelines for the appropriate use of standardized tests."[5]

Standardized assessments give only a snapshot of what a student knows (or does not know) on a given day. This snapshot is not panoramic. It does not give an expansive view of all that a student has achieved. Instead, it is a singular glimpse of an isolated skill or set of skills. Pitting assessment against achievement and allowing, by force of law and regulation of practice, assessment to be the all-time victor is not only counterintuitive, it is alo harmful to large populations of children—especially those children without the cultural capital to thrive under such alleged conditions of learning. Hoover and Shook assert that the tests that drive the school report card rankings and categorizations are actually tests of cultural capital and knowledge constructed within the microculture of the student's lived experience. In the case of reform-based accountability, it is the cultural knowledge (language, meanings, and experiences) of the upper economic class that is assessed by the tests that drive school report rankings. The tests and the school report cards sort children by economic class and subsequently rank the effectiveness of the educators who school them by assessing the knowledge kids have constructed from their particular lived experiences. There is tremendous disparity between the upper and lower economic classes in terms of knowledge and language meanings constructed from the widely differing opportunities and experiences encountered during childhood and adolescence.[6]

The Invisible Man

Eleven-year-old Jenny has muscular dystrophy and must use several communication devices in order to participate in a conversation and to evidence her intellectual understanding of her school curriculum. It would be educational malpractice for her school system to deny her any of the tools that she needs to display her learning. It would be unlawful to force

Jenny to take a paper-and-pencil standardized assessment and then to penalize her for poor performance. Retaining Jenny because she did not have an appropriate forum in which to display her achievement would be deleterious to her. In short, accommodations in assessment are appropriately made for those individuals with visible or documented handicaps. Why, then, do we fail to recognize the ever present hand of poverty as it waves to us from all corners of our world?

Perhaps it is because we are loath to label poverty as a handicap. There are too many tales of good Americans pulling themselves up by their proverbial bootstraps and becoming productive, even wealthy, citizens. To label poverty as a handicap is to bring it up against the American dream where it cannot peaceably exist. When one looks at the positive academic efforts made with poor students by instructors like Jaime Escalante and Lou Anne Johnson, it somehow does a disservice to a student to diminish expectation in the face of societal stresses. People of privilege fear that in acknowledging poverty, we are making easy excuses for both children and teachers. In part, this is because hope is abundant in the lens of privilege. Those who have little must fight harder to glimpse the American dream that is the American reality for most policymakers. There is often little hope in the lens of a poor minority child ensconced in an overwhelming atmosphere of familial distress.

Jonathan Kozol's pen gives voice to the words from an adolescent girl from the South Bronx: "Do you ever hear of cities that existed long ago and are extinct today?" asks Isabel. "I believe that this will happen here. Everyone will get so sick of life in Harlem and the South Bronx that we'll just give up and move to somewhere else. But it will be the same thing there again until the new place is so sad and ugly that it's destroyed and then we'll move on again to somewhere else, and somewhere else, until the whole world is destroyed and there is nothing to look back on but ashes."[7]

It is not that poverty is completely overlooked. It is written about, reported on, and placed neatly into bundles of quantifiable statistics.

It is often treated coldly, like a terse coroner's report, devoid of the feeling that may be engendered by the grim reality. Most of us are taught, at young ages, to avoid the eyes of the beggar on the street. We are taught subtle justifications for avoidance. "Those" people are criminals. They are drunkards. They simply don't want to work. But what of the 20 percent of the eighteen million people living in poverty in the United States who are children? Are they, too, deserving of our averted eyes and biased judgments? Perhaps we ignore the implications of poverty because acknowledging them would invoke a call to action that we are uncomfortable taking. In his works on social conscience, Friar Greg Cooney offers that once a person reacts against a situation experienced as morally confrontative and negative, his immediate reaction is that this ought not be so, and should not be allowed to continue. The person must then take a stance: either to ignore the experience or to heed the call of conscience and become personally involved. For such a call of conscience to crystallize, a nonnegotiable basis for it must be found, otherwise it is likely to remain nothing more than a future item of agenda. Achieving nonnegotiable status requires that the basis be beyond further questioning; to be an absolute that makes a permanent, irrefutable claim upon the individual.[8]

Ningún Probar, Por Favor (No Testing, Please)

Just as there are achievement and learning gaps for the invisible poor, there are also children whom policymakers and high stakes advocates refuse to hear. Some percent of all students in public schools have limited English proficiency. Such students are most often placed on the quick track to curricular conformity. They are expected to assimilate quickly and to begin to speak and read English within precisely structured timelines. They are fed into the high-stakes testing wringer with the mandate of demonstrating adequate yearly progress. They are given *accommodations* together with their testing. Semantically, an accommodation is different from a modification. To accommodate is to do a favor for, to modify is to adapt to needs. The most common accommodations are the removal of time constraints, use of a bilingual dictionary, and translation of the test itself. Voilà! A few remedial measures for those less fortunate and the law makers can boast that the test is truly color- and culture-blind. Right? Wrong!

First, consider the mind-set of accommodation, modification, or remediation. To receive any of these, one must somehow be "less." Less bright. Less articulate. Less acclimated. Less informed. Less testable. Too often, we do not think of our English Language Learning (ELL) students as gifted; we see only that they cannot learn in the language available to them. They are not tested on their own life experiences, on the cultural and historical content they have learned prior to entering the United States. They are tested on "our" homogenous history. The minds of ELL students are invalidated because their true voices are not heard. We expect them to be the needy rather than the needed in our classrooms.

Several students at an Arizona middle school made the headlines of their local paper. One student told police that her teacher demanded "that they [the students] speak English only and that if they do speak Spanish, they get yelled at." Another student said that she was hit "with an open hand and told not to speak Spanish but to speak in English."[9] There were similar complaints among other students. An article from the 1950s, perhaps? After all, such practices were common in the 1950s. The fact that this article appeared in 2004 only serves as an appalling affirmation that discrimination is thriving. The sanctions inherent in failed high-stakes assessments will exacerbate the injustices faced by throngs of young children each day in American classrooms.

Then, too, there are those children who have had no opportunity to learn before entering the United States. Their young lives have been fraught with overwhelming hardship. They have experienced hunger and witnessed death. They have seen their parents cry far more times than they have heard them laugh. They sleep on hard floors at home each night, without pillows and nightlights. And they are grateful because at least, at last, they are safe. They are in the land of opportunity. If only they are able to pass the test that will let them seize it.

There is little use in providing a translated version of a test of academic achievement for a child who has never received instruction in that language. It is not an accommodation to hand an illiterate child a dictionary—even one written in his native tongue. Allowing more time for the painstaking process of translating an assessment simply takes time away from the learning and the sharing that the child could be experiencing within a classroom. Accepted research in English as a Second Language (ESL) maintains that an ELL student needs between five and seven years of assisted English instruction before he or she is ready for the decontextualized academic English needed to be successful in the classroom setting and pass most academic tests.[10] In many states, English Language Learners are given a one-year grace period before they are expected to pass a standardized test. This is not only an injustice to the students, their families, and their school districts—it is a mockery of the meaning of grace.

Killing Me Softly

In *Uphill Both Ways,*[11] I reiterate the story of a seventh-grade at-risk student who had tears in her eyes as she asked me, "When I fail this test, like I know I will, will you call the test company and tell them that I'm smart?" I then tell of my eighth-grade students who were more practical than philosophical. They shrugged often and expressed gratefulness that testing got them out of homework. They filled in their answers rapidly and laid their heads on their desks. They doodled. They drew. And they didn't care. Whether it was the onset of teenage angst or the compilation of years of testing that they'd long ago deemed useless, the disenfranchisement was palpable. The vicious cycle of high-stakes testing is not limited to the poor or the culturally unassimilated. Nontraditional learners, too, of all races and all economic backgrounds are bullied by the paper-and-pencil abominations that fail to tell the truth about what they value and what they know. Test scores or other types of isolated numerical data are not justifications for making poor decisions. For instance, consider Edron. Edron is in third grade. His IQ is 160. This means that Edron's capacity for intellectual reasoning is above that of 99.9 percent of the population. Is it appropriate, however, to whisk this eight-year-old to a college campus? How far ahead in social maturity would the group that Edron surpasses in intellectual ability be? Would the chasm be navigable?

Consider, too, Aimee. Aimee is also in third grade. She is a gifted artist as well as a popular student. She has a deep sensitivity to the needs of others and is concerned about issues of fairness in the classroom. She is articulate and seems to always be speaking up for the underdog. Aimee failed her standardized reading and math tests. Is it appropriate to retain her? Or will her intuitive and interpersonal gifts be sacrificed in the process of retention?

Then there's Norisha. Norisha is in third grade, too. She doesn't stand out in the crowd. She tries her hardest to blend into the woodwork. School is difficult for her and her mother really doesn't believe in homework. She's often tired because she is home alone until her mother's shift at the hospital ends at 11 P.M. Will retention or other assessment-related sanctions improve the environmental conditions that affect her test-taking abilities?

Finally, Lynden provides a whirlwind of activity to his third-grade classroom. He is always out of his seat, rarely finishes his work, and talks back to the teacher whenever he's confronted. He is unpopular with the other students. His bossy attitude and his frequent classroom disruptions cause them to both fear and resent him. The class work that Lynden chooses to do demonstrates that he has satisfactory skills in reading. His intellect does not appear significantly different from that of his peers. However, the numbers associated with his standardized tests call for retention. His teacher rubs her temples, wondering if another year in school can possibly do any good for this already disenfranchised eight-year-old.

Do no harm. Whenever I teach the concepts of character education to teachers, "Do no harm" is among the first adages that we discuss. The above scenarios describe four very different students. It is quite possible that all four students could be in the same third-grade classroom and thus take the same standardized tests. Sorting those students according to their test scores alone does more than harm, it encourages the practice of educational mensacide. The fragile mind of a child can be permanently damaged by the poor decisions made in the name of conformity. It is educational malpractice to insist upon quantifying human beings. Author Alexandre Dumas offers, "All human wisdom is summed up in two words—wait and hope."[12] Genuine educational equity reflects both the ability to grow children and to give them vision. Growth is unpredictable; developmental milestones are not in lockstep. When we do not wait, we do harm. When we consistently use numbers to retaliate against learners limited by personal, societal, or environmental conditions, we preserve the greatest educational injustice of all—the deprivation of hope.

The Good Old Days

In researching practices in the area of assessment, I came across a table that showed the alleged progress of assessment. In 1993, in apparently kinder educational times, the following ideas were placed into the column of negative past practices:

- Placing more emphasis on what students could not or should not do
- Failing students who do not meet preset expectations for behavior or ability to do tasks
- Using pencil/paper tasks as the main way of assessing and evaluating students
- Comparing learners to each other

- Using checklists for students' report cards
- Excluding students from the assessment and evaluation process[13]

I was startled. Past practices? These are exactly the rituals that have been in place since the passing of the No Child Left Behind Act and the ensuing mandate of high-stakes assessment. Is it simply the sway of the educational pendulum that drives us to return to what didn't work once before? Or is it something more insidious and with deeper roots? It seems the pendulum has not acted of its own accord, but rather has been given a large political push. The financial growth of both textbook companies and the producers of standardized testing materials has been exponential since the adoption of the NCLB plan. According to Peter Sacks, author of *Standardized Minds: The High Price of America's Testing Culture and What We Can Do to Change It*, between 1960 and 1989 sales of standardized tests to public schools more than doubled, while enrollment increased only 15 percent.[14] Over the past five years alone, state testing expenditures have almost tripled, from $141 million to $390 million, according to Achieve Inc., a standards-movement group formed by governors and CEOs. Under the new legislation, as many as fifteen states might need to triple their testing budgets.[15]

Test prep and textbook moguls now stand as lobbyists with administrators and teachers. In fact, there has always been representation from these groups in government. The difference is that now their collective voice is much stronger. Where has this newfound power emanated from? Many critics of the Bush administration's educational politics point to a three-generation affiliation between the Bush family and the McGraw family. The McGraws, of course, are the proprietors of the McGraw-Hill Company and are responsible for the promotion and production of many of the aforementioned textbooks and tests. While I am hard pressed to lean toward political fanaticism, there is a noteworthy level of back-pocket favoritism apparent between the Bushes and the McGraws. Harold

McGraw Jr. sits on the national grant advisory and founding board of the Barbara Bush Foundation for Family Literacy. McGraw in turn received the highest literacy award from the first President Bush in the early 1990s for his contributions to the cause of literacy. The McGraw Foundation awarded Education Secretary Rod Paige its highest educator's award while Paige was Houston's school chief; Paige, in turn, was the keynote speaker at McGraw-Hill's "government initiatives" conference last spring. Harold McGraw III was selected as a member of President George W. Bush's transition advisory team, along with McGraw-Hill board member Edward Rust Jr., the CEO of State Farm Insurance and an active member of the Business Roundtable on educational issues. An ex–chief of staff for Barbara Bush is returning to work for Laura Bush in the White House—after a stint with McGraw-Hill as a media relations executive. John Negroponte left his position as McGraw-Hill's executive vice president for global markets to become Bush's ambassador to the United Nations.[16]

The profit margins for increased testing are steep and any endeavor that serves to line a pocket with green will not soon disappear—especially not when that enterprise can be marketed as an accountability measure to save America's failing schools. The deluge of press that tells us that we are demoralizing children and deprofessionalizing teachers seems like sour grapes to most. In *None of Our Business*,[17] I cite the many events that led to the standards revolution. Chief among these was the 1983 release of *A Nation at Risk*. This document, more than any other, defined the alleged need for avuncular corporate interest in American schools. The road to a standardized America, however, is paved with good intentions. Forcing "accountability" into public schools seemed like sound educational practice. After all, with increased corporate alliance and interest, it is important to show that learning is taking place. Otherwise, how will policymakers and other financial stakeholders know that they are getting the best bang for their educational bucks?

The dilemma comes not in making schools accountable, but in the measure of that accountability. Schools have always been answerable to a public demand. At their inception, schools were responsible for bringing a largely immigrant citizenship together for the purpose of creating idealized Americans who were capable of contributing to an increasingly global society. Respectful, literate learners who could perform the basic tasks of labor, production, and distribution were acceptable outcomes in a pretechnological society. However, one startling posttechnology claim is that the average worker today receives more information in a day than the average worker in 1900 did in a lifetime.[18] Under these circumstances, accountability loses some of its innocence and becomes a large net, a virtual "catchall" for special interest groups, politicians, profit-seekers, and media. In his book, *Accountability in Action*,[19] Douglas Reeves asserts that while accountability is definitely here to stay, the problem is that accountability, as it is presently practiced, is rarely meaningful and is often destructive. Reeves offers a three-point plan toward more effective accountability systems in schools.

First, accountability must include "cause and effect" variables. The effect variables are generally clear. These are things like test scores, attendance rates, drop-out rates, and so on. The cause variables are more subtle and include those practices in a school that directly influence student achievement. The cause variables promote a more holistic view, holding the system, rather than the child, responsible for the outcomes of assessment. Wholistic accountability embraces the concept that we must have a systematic review of all of the factors critical to a student's success in school—classroom performance assessments, curriculum, instructional practices, leadership strategies, parent involvement, and societal impacts.

Second, Reeves maintains that accountability systems must be accurate. Many accountability systems use data from test scores to evaluate teachers, curricula, and programs even when the test scores are from students who were not exposed to the teachers, curricula, and programs being evaluated. Reeves compares this to a medical experiment that evaluates a drug based upon the health of patients who did not take the drug.

Third, accountability systems must be designed to improve student achievement, not to embarrass, humiliate, or terrorize students and adults in the system. Wholistic, accurate, and proactive. These words bring to mind the pattern of assessment that was developing among public schools before the invasion of the NCLB rhetoric. The nineties showed teachers tiptoeing toward rubrics, increasing classroom performance assessments that reflected the range of multiple intelligences, and developing districtwide portfolio assessment procedures that reflected an array of student learning. Colleges and universities across the country began to move away from a reliance on SAT and ACT scores and allowed a greater expanse of criteria for admission to higher education. Then along came the sanctions. The nationwide "report cards." The notion that parents ought to flee from increasingly unsafe and academically irresponsible schools. With a signature, a policy became a prophecy.

The aftermath of the NCLB plan has brought more than educational inequity. It has brought a perverse view of assessment that permeates both sides of the "testing" camps. First, assessment's true purpose is viciously maligned by single-score indicators of success. Assessment becomes the Cyclops: myopic, unreasonable, and powerful. Those in the first camp, who envision high stakes to mean improved performance, are trapped in a numbers game whose only winners can ultimately be those students with the most cultural capital. On the other hand, for those in the second camp, assessment has become a bad word. I am reminded of a time when, interviewing for jobs, I would not utter the phrase "outcomes-based education" for fear of being immediately judged by the interviewing team. This is not because having outcomes or goals was considered poor policy, but rather because the movement toward outcomes took on a life of its own and became a vehicle for politics rather than practice.

In general, assessment refers to any activity undertaken by a student and a teacher to measure learning. Teachers would be remiss if they stumbled blindly through a curriculum, unaware of their students' progress. One of my college math professors comes to mind as I type this statement. He spent each of our classes with his back to his students, scribbling furiously on the chalkboard, highlighting a theorem, solving an equation, or elucidating some mathematical process or another. I didn't understand a word he said or a number that he wrote. I sat in my desk, trapped, while my already gargantuan math-induced insecurities were affirmed. I knew that the man with his back turned to me would also assess me. A fellow student, perhaps noting my deer-in-the-headlights look of terror, offered to tutor me in the evenings. I learned math that year, and I passed the assessments given, but my learning and my assessment were really incompatible creatures, gelling just enough that I "got by." My college math instructor was performing irresponsible assessment because it was matched to a poorly delivered curriculum. It is important to note that it was not the assessment itself that was in error, but rather the methodology employed.

Do You Know What I Know?

There are really two ways of looking at assessment—summative and formative. Summative assessment is the attempt to summarize student learning at some point, typically at the end of a period of instruction. Most standardized tests are summative. They are not designed to provide the major, contextualized feedback useful for helping teacher and student during the learning process. Formative assessment, on the other hand, occurs when teachers feed information back to students in ways that enable the students to learn better or when students can engage in similar, self-reflective processes. Assessment becomes formative when the evidence gained from the testing is used to adapt the teaching to meet student needs. If the primary purpose of assessment is to support high-quality learning, then formative assessment ought to be understood as the most important assessment practice.[20]

Paul Black and Dylan William researched the best practices in the area of formative assessment in 1998. Dylan and William found that to be truly helpful to the students, formative information should be focused on the task, not the student; and the student must understand the feedback in order to make use of it.[21] Effective feedback allows students to express their understanding, contains classroom dialogue that focuses on enhancing understanding, and includes specific guidance on how to improve performance.[22]

I was watching my son play one of his PlayStation 2 games the other day. His goal was to pass through a series of scenic areas with increasingly difficult navigation. On his first level, there were several "helpful hint" sections where he was able to get effective guidance from one of the game's many characters. That first level was fairly short, too, enabling him to feel success. The second and third levels were a bit more complex and he more frequently "died" and had to begin anew. There was an important factor worked into the game, though—at each point where he failed, he only needed to go back as far as his last portion of mastery. In other words, once he had traversed the jungle portion of level two with success, he did not have to repeat that performance. He needed only return to the subject matter that he had not yet mastered.

My son, like most of the students whom I work with, has a very short attention span. How is it then, that in a game overrun with frequent prescriptions for failure, he maintains focus and attention for extended periods of time? Part of the reasoning, to be sure, is the ever changing visual field and the amount of challenge that the game serves to his stubborn nature. Akin to those features, though, is the system of feedback and reward that are woven seamlessly into the game's program. With ongoing corrective feedback, he is given the opportunity to modify his behavior to experience increasingly greater levels of success. Who would have thought that an answer to the assessment dilemma was embedded into a twelve-year-old's recreation?

This We Believe

Creating a culture of success is indispensable to formative assessment. A culture of success is one in which teachers believe that all students are capable of achieving. While formative assessment can help all pupils, it yields particularly good results with low achievers by concentrating on specific problems with their work and giving them a clear understanding of what is wrong and how to put it right. Students can accept and work with such messages, provided that they are not clouded by overtones about ability, competition, and comparison with others.[23]

The Dimensions of Learning Model[24] states that attitudes and perceptions affect students' ability to learn. For example, if students view the classroom as an unsafe and disorderly place, they will likely learn little there. Similarly, if students have negative attitudes about classroom tasks, they will probably put little effort into those tasks. A key element of effective instruction, then, is helping students to establish positive attitudes and perceptions about the classroom and about learning. In fact, the DOL model maintains that no meaningful instruction can take place in the absence of relationship. Once a culture focused on learning paired with success is established, only then can students acquire new knowledge and extend and generalize that knowledge to other areas of curriculum. Once students are able to use knowledge meaningfully, they then develop the habits of mind to continue on a quest for lifelong learning.

Formative assessment relies as much on student self-assessment as it does on practical teacher feedback. Pupils are generally honest and reliable in assessing both themselves and one another; they can even be too hard on themselves. The main problem is that pupils can assess themselves only when they have a sufficiently clear picture of the targets that their learning is meant to attain. Unfortunately, many pupils do not have such a picture, and they appear to have become accustomed to receiving classroom teaching as an arbitrary sequence of exercises with no overarching rationale. To overcome this pattern of passive reception requires hard and sustained work. When pupils do acquire such an overview, they then become more committed and more effective as learners. Moreover, their own assessments become an object of discussion with their teachers and with one another, and this discussion further promotes the reflection on one's own thinking that is essential to good learning.[25]

To create a culture of success, assessment must focus on meaningful performances. It must help students to draw out their strengths, rather than focusing on weaknesses alone. Linda Darling-Hammond is a researcher who has studied the use of authentic and performance-based assessments and their wide-ranging influence on school culture and improvement. Darling-Hammond states, "The more information teachers obtain about what students know and think as well as how they learn, the more capacity they have to reform their pedagogy, and the more opportunities they create for student success."[26]

Formative, performance-based assessment is instrumental in providing equity among learners. Assessment for its intended purpose is unfair if 1) students are not provided with equal opportunities to demonstrate what they know, 2) these biased assessments are used to judge students' capabilities and needs, and 3) these distorted views of students are used to make educational decisions that ultimately lead to limitations of educational opportunities for them.[27]

I had the opportunity to serve on the reading committee for the awarding of a prestigious financial scholarship to assist graduating seniors with their transition to college. Financial need was not a factor of the scholarship. On paper, the selection process seemed to be without bias. As I read over the first few applications, I was impressed with the caliber of the student questionnaires and with the writing abilities that were reflected not only among their personal essays but also within the bodies of the reference letters that had been written on each student's behalf. It was only after reading through several scholarship applications that I began to notice subtle discrepancies. Some students, most of whom reflected a level of financial need within their applications, had worked more jobs throughout high school and thus reflected less extracurricular participation. This had a negative impact upon their overall scores. Some students, too, professed to be in the first generation of children in their family to be able to attend college. Often their reference letters (one of which was required to be from a family friend), while just as much from the heart as all the others, were less articulate and expansive. This, too, had a negative impact on the final score. A tool that was carefully crafted to equalize applicants could not really perform its function. Separation and segregation were waiting in the background and were affected by that timeless tyrant, cultural capital.

Assessment can only be appropriate for students when it is individualized, formative, performance based, and part of an ongoing cycle. In the classroom, I tell my students to "Plan-Do-Check-Act" (PDCA). That is, they must decide what to do, do it, examine the results garnered, and make changes to secure an even more productive outcome on their next trial. It seems that we, as educational leaders, ought to follow the same prescription. When we plan for assessment, and then carry it out, we must check to be sure that we are accurately measuring all that a student can do. When that assessment tells us time and again that instead of increasing learning we are engaging in hope-deprivation, we must act. Consider the conclusion of this chapter a call to action. Do not allow the will of students, or your own wills, to be damaged by a system in need of repair. Rather than fear the repercussions of the sanctions that accompany the test, get involved. Send your voice and your protest to the policymakers and politicians who hold the purse strings. Rather than trying to force square pegs into round holes, find a puzzle board that will allow for the unique traits of all. Celebrate the successes in your classroom, for they are many. And most of all, give your students a reason to celebrate, too. Assessment for learning. Assessment for progress. Assessment for hope.

CHAPTER THREE

Inequity Within Standards

Acceptance of prevailing standards often means we have no standards of our own.

—Jean Toomer[1]

Chutes and Ladders

As a psychology major in college, I decided to do an experiment that involved determining a rat's ability to navigate a maze while being influenced by two different types of music. My hypothesis was that the soothing tones of classical music would motivate the rats to complete the maze even faster than the culinary enticements they were given in the control phase of the process. Secondary to this, I further hypothesized that the rats that were exposed to raucous heavy metal music would have difficulty finding their way through the maze, even having previously mastered it sans song. As it turned out, my hypothesis was wrong. The rats that listened to the heavy metal music did far better than the rats listening to classical music. Instead of being soothed, the rats exposed to classical music seemed frightened, hovering near the entrance of the maze, not even cajoled to action by the foods that had worked to train them in the past.

What had gone wrong? I turned to my professor for assistance. He listened to the pieces of music that I had chosen and pointed out the heavy concentration of violins in the classical selection. Violins, it seems, emulate the stress-cry of rats. The rats that heard the classical music were not soothed—they were distressed. The rats were unable to perform as they had been trained to because they were afraid. With the absence of the music, the rats were once again able to successfully complete the maze.

This leads me to wonder. What kind of music are today's youth being forced to face? Are there conditions of learning that cause such intense fear that students cannot carry out even those jobs that they have been well prepared to perform? Consider, for example, the six thousand students in Massachusetts who earned all the requirements for graduation except passing the state's MCAS (Massachusetts Comprehensive Assessment System) exam.[2] Those six thousand students did not join their peers in June of 2003 as they walked across the stage. They did not receive congratulations from their families. They did not have the same higher education opportunities as the people lucky enough to pass all of the sections of the MCAS. These students, had, in fact, failed the MCAS five times. Yet they were able to demonstrate learning in other ways. Perhaps the absence, not of classical music, but of classical standardized assessment, would have enabled those students to become something other than inappropriately judged and subsequently demoralized.

It is difficult to separate educational standards from standardized assessment. The mandates imposed by the No Child Left Behind Act have united them into a shotgun-wedding approach to educating children. It's a polygamous union, too. In some states, like Wisconsin, there are over five hundred state standards that must be wed to assessment. Robert Marzano, senior fellow at the Mid-continent Regional Education Library (McREL) in Aurora, Colorado, studied the standards around the country and found it would take twenty-three years of schooling to cover all of the benchmarks. "Teachers can't teach it all," he says, "and kids couldn't possibly learn it all."[3]

We often speak of standards as if for many years they simply didn't exist until suddenly, one day, under the light of a political fire, they came to life. While it's true that the current movement did get its start from a political event in the form of President George H. W. Bush's 1989 education summit, it is equally true that curriculum, by every other name, has smelled as sweet since the beginning of time.

I remember the summer before second grade. I knew that second grade was going to be a good year because I was going to learn to write in cursive. I knew that in third grade I'd learn the "times tables," and that in fourth grade I'd study the history of Wisconsin. The lessons designed in each of the preceding grades were part of a sequence of instruction that idealistically would enable me to be successful in each of my new endeavors. No one was talking about standards then. There wasn't a whisper of "outcomes-based education," either. Scope and sequence were on the scene but Madeline Hunter was only just beginning to have her way with them. "Teaching for transfer" was all the rage, and instructors everywhere were seeking real-life applications for instruction. Developing the ability to generalize learning was considered as important as the learning itself.

Now we speak of a "standards and accountability movement." The implications of that bother me. Certainly, it is fitting to move toward any curricular practice that enables a teacher to reach a wide variety of learners and to provide a common set of skills that are either marketable or necessary in today's world. I am bothered by the implication of the word *movement* and by its kindred cousin *reform*. Historically speaking, "movements" have arisen out of great injustices. There was the women's movement that sought the power to vote and the power of equalization in the workplace. There was the civil rights movement that sought to end discrimination and to promote acceptance and respect. The semantic insinuation associated with the "standards and accountability movement" is that we are chartering new territory in the name of children who must be rescued from their current failing and unsafe learning environments.

The Big Rocks

Let's approach standards from another direction. First, let's assume that it is not children who fail within a learning environment but rather that the learning environment fails to meet the needs of some children. Our best practices with regard to standards, then, must focus on the conditions of learning rather than on the conditions of life experienced by children. It should not matter that a child is black, or poor, or a kinesthetic learner. It also should not matter that a child is white, wealthy, and an auditory learner. A commentary entitled "Why Standards: Equity for All Students" addresses this issue with the notion that "a dysfunctional education system—that helps only some Americans acquire skills and knowledge to be successful—leads to a dysfunctional society. For both a strong democracy and a strong economy, people need to be more literate, more technologically savvy and informed than ever before. An education system that prepares students so unevenly for the world doesn't bode well for our collective future."[4]

Author Douglas Reeves emphasizes the advantages of shifting away from standards as a legal mandate and toward standards as a foundation for fairness, success, and respect. Both Reeves and Larry Ainsworth, director of the Center for Performance Assessment, are proponents of a "power standards" model of curriculum delivery. Using a power standards model means first identifying those standards that are the most critical for success in subsequent grades in school. When I think about the concept of power standards, I am reminded of the story of a college professor who placed a dozen fist-sized rocks into a bucket. When the bucket was filled to the top and no more rocks would fit inside, he asked, "Is this bucket full?" Everyone in the class said, "Yes." Then he said, "Really?" He reached under the table and pulled out a bucket of gravel. Then he dumped some gravel in and shook the bucket, causing pieces of gravel to work themselves down into the spaces between the big rocks. Then he smiled and asked the group once more, "Is the bucket full?" By this time the class was onto him. "Probably not," one of them answered. "Good!" he replied. And he reached under the table and brought out a bucket of sand. He started dumping the sand in and it went into all the spaces left between the rocks and the gravel. Once more he asked the question,

"Is this bucket full?" "No!" the class shouted. Once again he said, "Good!" Then he grabbed a pitcher of water and began to pour it in until the bucket was filled to the brim. Then he looked up at the class and told them the point of his illustration: If you don't put the big rocks in first, you'll never get them in at all.

Any teacher who is a committed professional can tell you what the "big rocks" are in the realm of standards. The ability to decode words, for example, is a critical skill. Knowledge of the basic underlying processes in mathematics is necessary for continued success in math. It is crucial that older students understand the mentality of discrimination that preceded enslavement in America or the Holocaust in Germany. It is only with understanding that history's mistakes are not repeated. It is only fitting, then, that the process of identifying power standards should be directed by those who have the most to gain from having well-prepared and capable learners—classroom teachers.

It seems simple. All we really need to do is to ask three basic questions.

- First, what essential understandings and skills do our students most need?
- Second, which standards can be clustered or incorporated into others?
- Third, what do students need for success in school, in life, and on the high-stakes measures that currently exist?[5]

Unfortunately, solving the issues associated with standards is not as uncomplicated as it seems to be. I am getting a picture in my head of Lucille Ball, dressed in her crisp white apron, poised to work on the assembly line at a candy factory. As anyone who's ever watched Nick at Nite knows, Lucy's apron doesn't stay white for long and her attitude certainly doesn't remain chipper. In short, by the end of the episode, Lucy is in panic mode, unable to deal with the pace of the candy as it rolls down the line. She is messy, overwhelmed, and unable to do the job for which she was hired. Because it's a TV show and because we all love Lucy, we are able to have a laugh at her expense. It is not funny, however, that educational standards seem to have created the same panic in teachers that those innocent chocolates created for Lucy. Albert Einstein is quoted as saying that problems cannot be solved using the same mentality under which they were created, and he's absolutely right. Many teachers are tired and overwhelmed by the onslaught of demands placed upon them. They are told that unless they are able to teach *all* of the standards assigned to their grade level, they are failing at their work. I believe that it is a "Post-Traumatic Standards Disorder" that is obscuring the view of the forest for the trees and preventing the implementation of the power standards that are truly good for kids.

Author George Madaus sensed the eventual onset of Post-Traumatic Standards Disorder in 1994. His words reflect both the condition and the cure.

> I believe that any proposed exam system simply cannot produce truly "just" measures until policymakers put in place appropriate national delivery standards (e.g., conditions; inputs; processes; funding needed for social, health, family and educational resources; and support systems). Therefore, in addressing the equity of alternative assessments in a high-stakes, policy-driven exam system, policy must be crafted that first and foremost creates a level playing field for students and schools. Only then can the claim be made that a national examination system is an equitable technology for making decisions about individuals, schools, or districts.[6]

The idea of "delivery standards" will be addressed by examining the best practices associated with equity in Chapter 5. Appropriate delivery, however, will only solve part of the complex stress affiliated with standards. Another formidable foe is that for many individuals the very idea of standardization is anathema to what it means to be a free-thinking American. For example, in *Do the Standards Go Far Enough? Power, Policy, and Practice in Mathematics Education*, Michael

Apple raises concerns about the standards for mathematics written by the National Council for Teachers of Mathematics.

Apple raises an important point in advising the community of education reform to be aware of the dangers of setting common expectations when the starting points for children in our country are so widely varied. Concerns about the financial crisis in education, the nature of inequality in schools, and the power of mathematical knowledge in our economy all are cause to caution that "without a deeper understanding . . . the *Standards* will be used in ways that largely lend support to the conservative agenda for educational reform."[7]

In an article for *Education Week* entitled "Leaving No Child Behind," Donald Gratz, a senior associate on national school reform for the Community Training and Assistance Center in Boston, points out that there is a huge chasm between *expecting* every child to learn and *requiring* that success. Standards and expectations, while often used interchangeably, are not the same thing. We can't legislate that teachers expect more, only that they require more.[8]

I am taken back in time to the required reading lists that were on the syllabi of so many of my graduate classes. In the beginning, I would dutifully purchase all of the books and begin to read all of them, even those that failed to capture my interest or my intellect. After a few classes, however, I was able to see that requirement and expectation were only loosely linked to the actual curriculum of most classes. Most professors wanted only sections of books, especially those that reflected their own rhetoric, fed back to them. I learned that I could meet the expectation by checking a copy of the book out of the library and skimming it for the analogies that supported the professor's remarks in class.

I am thinking, too, of the questions that appear at the ends of chapters in textbooks for my students. Often, those questions are assigned with the expectation that the students will read the chapter and discover the answers. However, the only real requirement of the assignment is that students find the correct answers regardless of whether they actually read the assignment or not.

Developing ongoing products, then, rather than end products should be the goal of education. Citing the 1968 Rosenthal experiment in which teachers, told that some students were more capable than others, consequently had higher expectations of (and received higher results from) those students, Gratz maintains that expectations are the true catalysts for learning. He states that standards require the most progress from students with the farthest to go. Without extra help and time, such a requirement may not be realistic or fair. Extra time is essential for a standards-based system, but new time-based schools giving students that extra time have not emerged to replace our age-based ones. If we, as a nation, are going to enforce higher standards with high-stakes tests and deny diplomas to students who can't pass them, we should be honest about our intentions and drop the self-righteous language about leaving no child behind. Standards with age-specific, high-stakes tests are about punishments, not expectations.[9]

Time is not the only factor that affects standards. Time's consistent counterpart, money, also has a direct impact on the success of the requirements *and* the expectations placed upon children. Consider Figure One.[10] Inequities obviously exist between two schools located within miles of one another in the Milwaukee School District. And they are not only the unequal conditions imposed by society, but also the inequality of funding between the two schools. These are unfair measures imposed by the very system that purports to educate all of its learners! While factors such as excellent teaching, innovative programming, and strong leadership are obviously necessary to a school district's success, these factors are ultimately contingent upon a district's financial resources. Fewer financial resources signify reduced learning opportunities and unbalanced access to high-quality education. Inequitable allocation of these vital financial resources has resulted in a state-sponsored system of educational discrimination in Wisconsin, where students in property-rich districts reap the benefits and students in property-poor districts suffer the consequences of demographics beyond their control.[11]

NICOLET

Enrollment in 1999–2000: 1,320

Spending per student 1998–99 in
  district: $12,674

Complete Annual School Cost;
  $11,120 Shared Cost.

Built: 1955, with additions in
  1962, 1968, and 1989

Total campus area: 15 acres

Total square feet of building:
  367,000

Total square feet of library and number of materials: Two libraries, 3,572 square feet and 4,752 square feet, with 45,000 books, videos, and other materials

Computers available for student
  use: 425

Average class size: 24

Average salary for teachers last
  year: $52,794

Percentage of last year's graduates
  who went to college: 92.1%

CUSTER

Enrollment in 1999–2000: 1,188

Spending per student 1998–99 in
  district: $8,344

Complete Annual School Cost;
  $6,555 Shared Cost.

Built: 1956

Total campus area: 4 acres

Total square feet of building:
  260,938

Total square feet of library and number of materials: 5,181 square feet with 17,701 books, videos, and other materials.

Computers available for student
  use: 400

Average class size: 25 to 30

Average salary for teachers last
  year: $47,189

Percentage of last year's graduates
  who went to college: 46%

Figure One. Nicolet vs. Custer

I don't know of any school district that employs MacGyver. Thus, it is ridiculous to expect and require that all children learn a common curriculum while providing some with enough desks and books and expecting the others to get by with only paperclips and string. What's more, most discussions about funding equity have focused only on the different levels of funding *between* districts, and it is often assumed that funds are distributed evenly to schools *within* districts. But recent research highlights startling differences within districts, with some schools receiving as much as 60 percent more funding than others with similar categories and numbers of students.[12] It is primarily urban schools that have higher concentrations of poor, minority, and at-risk students. There's even evidence that large concentrations of at-risk students within a school places all students attending the school, including those with no individual-level risk, at greater risk of academic failure.[13] John Beam, the executive director of the National Center for Schools and Communities at Fordham University, makes an excellent point when he asks, "If politicians and voters at the state and often district levels continue to be willing to underfund central-city public schools, how will the threat of losing a little more money, which, after all, is only for poor kids, motivate them?"[14]

A Puzzling Solution

After acknowledging the problems that are inherent in standards (lack of time to implement, lack of money to equalize implementation, forced uniformity, and an elementary confusion with expectations), it is important to realize that despite the obvious drawbacks, standards are here to stay. In *Uphill Both Ways,*[15] I discuss the building blocks that all students need to experience success. There are chapters dedicated to character education, to a constructivist curriculum, to multiple intelligences instruction, to a community-based approach, and to the relationship building that precedes any learning in a classroom. I touch on the idea of power standards and quip that before students can ingest academic standards, they must first have Abraham Maslow's "power" standards fulfilled. Students must have food, shelter, and relationships. I truly believe that students will only learn effectively and retain information appropriately when their basic needs are met. They may be able to spit back information on an empty stomach, and they may even be able to fill in the bubbles on a standardized test after sleeping in a shelter, but real learning—the impactful kind that determines the quality of a life rather than the quality of a test score—is dependent on the satisfaction of basic needs.

For the purposes of the remainder of this chapter, I am going to wave my magic wand and assume that there are equalized conditions of learning and that students have had enough basic needs sated that they are ready to learn. Many students across America, in fact, are ready to learn. They do come to school with enough food, clothing, supervision, and love. In Wisconsin, they come to school to face the five hundred–plus standards that someone has determined that they need. In other states, they wrangle with more or fewer standards. The point, of course, is that in today's schools, all students will encounter standards.

I think that the term "power standard" is brilliant. It resonates strength and expectations. It brings to mind power lunches and power walks. It connotes commitment, focus, and determination. The real beauty of it lies in its secret. If you promise not to tell any politicians, I'll tell you. *It's what we've always done.*

Maybe all teachers everywhere haven't used a common set of guiding principles to transition students from grade to grade and toward eventual graduation, but certainly most have. Perhaps there are a few scattered schools out there in which teachers have always been the sages on the stage who refuse to communicate with colleagues. I've never witnessed any of them and it seems as though they wouldn't thrive. Education has not been a closed-door enterprise for a very long time.

I've known some excellent cooks in my lifetime. Each of them has produced many tasty main dishes, several delicious desserts, and a satisfying variety of salads. They've even been able to meet my needs as a vegetarian. I've noticed an interesting phenomenon with these chefs. When I ask for a recipe, each of them pauses, wrinkles her face, and places a hand on her hip. "I don't exactly know," she says reflectively. "I just prepare it automatically, I've been making it so long." In order to really learn how to fix the dish, I would need to follow my friend around the kitchen, taking notes on ingredients and procedures.

It is the same way in education; we have many tenured teachers who long ago determined what skills were needed for each child to experience a successful transition to the next grade. Having developed the outline, these teachers spent years developing the materials and perfecting the delivery of their instruction. Many prepared learners were passed through the grades within a school. Less tenured staff have attempted to duplicate their efforts, often with positive results. However, as it is with recipes, some ingredients may have been missed. Over time, with new staff members working with students each year, education has experienced a dilemma of too many details competing with too little direction. In short, through a natural process (and an easily remedied one), we've lost some of the most elemental building blocks that were allowing children to experience successful transitions.

Amazingly, our answer to this has been to add more details. Think about it. Five hundred standards. Not only that, five hundred standards that claim to be testable standards. High-stakes testable standards. Not only do children need to be prepared for the next grade, but the test looms, providing us with Orwellian visions of sixteen-year-olds driving themselves to eighth grade. It is Lucy in the candy factory. It is Post–Traumatic Standards Disorder. It is feeling exhausted before education even gets under way.

Power standards are a means to mediate the politics of standards and to merge academic necessities comfortably back into an overwhelmed curriculum. Power standards are purposefully selected within and across the core areas so that educators can focus on the most critical targets for student learning, those that are essential for students to understand deeply. Power standards emphasize the "big ideas" and higher-order thinking. Grade-level benchmarks that are the building blocks toward the power standards need to clearly define what students would understand deeply as they pass from grade to grade. Power standards can also extend beyond core academic areas. For example, the American Association of School Libraries offers nine information literacy standards that include items such as "The student who is information literate accesses information effectively and efficiently and uses information accurately and creatively."[16]

Larry Ainsworth offers an eight-step process for identifying power standards. To me, the process resembles that of putting a jigsaw puzzle together. It would be very time consuming to use a trial-and-error method for putting a five-hundred-piece landscape puzzle together. Instead, most people first separate out the edges of the puzzle, grouping them by color or design. Next, all of the blue pieces for the sky are set aside, then the green of the grass, the golden hues of the wheat, and finally the deeper green of the forest. In this way, the puzzle can be made whole by putting together manageable chunks of information that already have something in common.

Ainsworth advocates for such an approach. He recommends the following steps:

- Begin with one subject and one grade in state or district standards
- Identify essentials for that subject (things students need to know in school, in life, and on high-stakes assessments)
- Review high-stakes testing information and guidelines, looking for links between what is in the curriculum and what's tested
- Revise your curriculum to include any key elements that seem to be missed
- Compare one grade's selections to the grade above and the grade below within that same grade span
- Identify gaps, overlaps, and omissions
- Make adjustments as needed in indicators to ensure the vertical "flow" within that grade span
- Once the power standards are identified in one grade span (K–2, 3–5, 6–8, or 9–12) make connections to other grade spans until you have a K–12 "flow" of essentials[17]

I think that the second bullet, the idea of identifying the *essentials*, is the most significant aspect of the infusion of power standards. It reminds me of a vacation that I took with a friend. When I went to pick her up to go to the airport, I had my one carry-on bag lying in a corner of the backseat. As we loaded her three bags, pillow, and over-stuffed purse into the car, I couldn't resist commenting that we were only going to be gone for a week. She looked at me seriously and threw her hands in the air, exclaiming, "Well, I only brought the essentials!"

When people are facing changes, human nature leads us to ask, "What about me?" Teachers ask this question often. We're territorial about it, too. I've been in many team meetings over the years and am still amazed when a teacher on the team argues against doing a developmentally appropriate, all-grade-level activity on "her" time as if forty more minutes of math will have more impact than a field trip to a wildlife sanctuary. The "me/my" mentality has driven the standards movement from practical to impractical over a very short period of time. It has become a Dr. Seuss Sneetches story, in which one department of educators looks over at another and exclaims, with dismay, "But now they have stars on thars!" Soon they run off to a departmental meeting and claim that they are losing the race. That the social studies people, or the language arts people, or the science people have more standards. They anticipate the argument that more standards will lead toward more dollars for that department. They quickly pick up their pens and draw "stars" on their own bellies, remembering a few more critical elements of their own curriculum that children must learn.

> Enter George W. McGraw McBean, who happens to drive a high-stakes testing machine.
> He welcomes them all, makes all teachers the same.
> Gives their students all numbers where they once had a name.
> He eyes all the standards, then shouts in elation!
> "Only a hundred dollars each for test preparation!"
> He distributes some workbooks, some pencils, (some lies),
> And he gives them advice which he tells them is wise.
> "Tell your students to eat right and to get enough rest,
> That's the best preparation for this high-stakes test!"

When he's stolen their paint sets (taken every last frill),
He retreats to the safety of Capitol Hill.
The teachers are left, with more work to do,
With less tools to teach, and with more students, too.

This, of course, doesn't have to be the end of the analogy. After all, in the lore of the Sneetches, Dr. Seuss taught this lesson: "Some had stars upon them, and they walked proud all about. But they soon learned it was okay with or without."[18] Doing what is best for students should not be about denying them recess. It should not be about sacrificing creativity for rote memorization. It certainly should not be about allocating budget dollars intended for the arts into more materials to teach those subjects most often covered on the high-stakes measures. It is crucial that power standards not be confused with "sole" standards; that is, that because certain aspects of a curriculum are emphasized, other elements are denied.

Teachers really are remarkable people. Whenever I do large group seminars, I am consistently impressed by the insights that educators across the United States are able to offer. When I go to share what I know, I always return home having learned something. Much of the negative literature about standards discusses the harm we are doing to our students when we fail to treat them as individuals. Author John Taylor Gatto offers, "Schools were designed by Horace Mann, E. I. Thorndike, and others to be instruments of the scientific management of a mass population. Schools are intended to produce, through the application of formulas, formulaic human beings whose behavior can be predicted and controlled."[19] In 1906, the new General Education Board formed by J. D. Rockefeller stated, in its mission, "In our dreams, people yield themselves with perfect docility to our molding hands."[20] Today, it seems that those "people" include teachers. Current legislation calls for docility and passivity. It tells us that we must accept that there are five hundred things that children "must" learn. In his book, *Re-Imagine!* Tom Peters relates, "Teacher training programs, a friend of mine deeply involved in them says, attract people who 'typically color inside the lines.' Sad. Yes, there are Great Teachers and Great Principals. But they fail to have much sustained impact on the entire system. Therein lies the problem. It isn't so in the private sector. When a 'revolutionary' comes along, a Dell, a Schwab, a Wal*Mart . . . the rest of the world stands up and takes notice . . . or gets beaned. In the school system, it's the 'revolutionary' who gets beaned."[21]

Sitting Bull is attributed with the notion that we must all put our minds together and see what kind of life we can make for our children. It will take all of our minds, all of our voices, and much of our hearts to do what should be done for children. It will mean determining what is essential, as Ainsworth indicates, not only for their schooling, but for their lives. It will mean accepting the artistry of those who color outside of the lines. It will mean putting issues of equity at the forefront. It will mean holding true to what we know instead of what we see.

In *Amazing Grace,* Jonathan Kozol tells of a section in the poorest part of the Bronx, where the city had painted murals on the highway sides of the dilapidated buildings. The director of a program for children in that area showed Kozol the paintings, commenting, "Nobody lives here. Those buildings are all empty." She went on to say that the city had the murals painted on the walls not for the people in the neighborhood—because they're facing the wrong way— but for the tourists and commuters. "The idea is that they mustn't be upset by knowing too much about the population here. It isn't enough that the people are sequestered. It's also important that their presence be disguised or sweetened. The city did not repair the buildings so that kids who live around here could, in fact, *have* pretty rooms like those. Instead they *painted* pretty rooms on the façade. It's an illusion."[22]

We must give the standards the power that they deserve so that all children can attain similar academic goals. We should not, however, allow standards to be the illusion that such goals are attainable in the same manner or at the same rate for all populations. Students in straight rows, in clean schools, seated with full stomachs at comfortable desks is a pretty picture. It is also an achievable picture. But it will take all of us, those with stars and those without, to make it into a reality.

CHAPTER FOUR

Inequity in Curriculum

If Hero means sincere man, why may not every one of us be a Hero?

—Thomas Carlyle[1]

One Fine Day

I watch my students argue over the dubious honor of being the student chosen to erase the board, or to write homework assignments upon it, or to take an important message down the short hallway to the office. There is real emotion in their voices as they vie for the privilege of being singled out. Even in seventh grade, each of them is on a relentless quest to be special. There is a deep-seated importance in recognition.

In fifth grade, my son was the champion of the pinewood car-racing contest that was part of the science curriculum. He received a trophy from his teacher—paper cups glued together and spray painted gold. He carried it home carefully, grinning broadly. He was proud of his achievement and his trophy sat upon his dresser long after one of the cups fell off, exposing its white underside. It did not matter to him that his trophy was not from a store. It mattered that it was from the heart. And the visual recognition of his accomplishment mattered most of all.

It is February and my weekly school communication informs me that it is Black History Month. I do a quick Internet search and find that the encyclopedia has more than thirty comprehensive topics devoted to "Black History," and there are hundreds of Web sites. I wonder why the many contributions of African Americans, and their heritage, are more important in February than they are in March or April or August. Is it equity that nine months of the school year are dedicated to European history? That, at best, black history shares space with the white male hegemony that holds dominion over the standards and the assessments in most classrooms? I look around my classroom and wonder about the heroes of my Hispanic students. I wonder who from the Hmong culture had influences in art, music, science, and literature. I wonder why there are not months dedicated to the entirety of the melting pot. Perhaps it is because there are not enough months. Perhaps it is because the history books have already been written. And perhaps it is because silence is affirmation and that with each textbook purchased and each worksheet copied, educators make choices about which aspect of the American legacy that they will idealize.

This chapter is about best practices among issues of literacy. It is not singularly about best practices for students of color, for children living in poverty, or for children with maladaptive family units. It is about using sound instructional strategies for *all* children. It would be remiss, however, to fail to direct specific commentary toward the aforementioned groups, because without best practice, these groups are the most likely to fail and the most likely to be deprived of hope.

I have a bit of reservation, too, as I type the words "best practice." So much has been written about the salvation of our schools, and so much has been labeled "best practice" that many teachers roll their eyes, close their classroom doors, and resign themselves to another swing of the educational pendulum. The suggestions given in this chapter are not meant to be prescriptions; they are, however, offered as time-tested strategies that have helped wide varieties of students to experience success in school. Consider each. Take what fits. Decline what doesn't. And when something that you do instructionally in your classroom isn't mentioned here, raise your hand at the next staff meeting and share it with your peers. Best practice is rooted both in what works and what is shared. Public education will not benefit from yet another commiseration about the problems that we have; but it will profit greatly from the collective knowledge that we share.

Where Do We Grow from Here?

I was at a meeting the other day and was discussing this book with the administrator of a large urban elementary school who was sitting next to me. I made a comment about how inner cities have far more severe issues than the suburban district that I worked in. She bristled a bit, immediately asking for clarification. I talked about the greater levels of poverty that she dealt with each day, the more severe behaviors, and the more disenfranchised families. She acknowledged that, indeed, urban schools had each of these on a greater scale because their overall population was much larger. I still felt defensiveness in the air, so I asked about it. It seems that she had heard some masked discrimination in my comments and she had expected that I was more willing to "write off" or have lesser expectations for urban youth because of their cultural or economic issues.

I hastily assured her that this was not the case. I have a deeply rooted belief that all children can learn. In fact, *Uphill Both Ways*[2] is dedicated to this philosophy and gives specific strategies for how to enact it. This is where the fine line between acknowledgment and knowledge becomes apparent. Acknowledgment of the current conditions of learning for many disadvantaged students, both urban and rural, must be given. Statistics must be shared. Reality must be addressed. However, all of this must be done with the knowledge that the data are not a promise for the future, and that the way things are is certainly not a reflection on the way things ought to be and can be.

According to the U.S. Department of Education's Common Core of Data, 40 percent of public schools in large cities are "intensely segregated," meaning more than 90 percent of the students are children of color. And 40 percent of all schools are "racially exclusive," with fewer than 10 percent students of color. In fact, racial segregation surpasses that which existed before the landmark *Brown v. Board of Education* Supreme Court decision in 1954.[3] Sixty-three percent of all white students go to schools that are 90–100 percent white. Black students in the South are only half as likely to attend intensely segregated schools as those who live in the Northeast. The most intense school segregation happens in large northern metropolitan areas surrounded by white suburbs. Students of color in rural areas and small towns are much more likely to attend integrated schools than those who live in large cities. Big metropolitan areas maintain school segregation by having smaller school districts. The 1974 Milliken Supreme Court decision forbids desegregation plans that cross school district lines, so if the suburbs and the city have separate districts, their students won't be able to attend the same schools.[4]

Much has been written in recent years, both pro and con, on the subject of resegregation. In *ColorLines*, a journal dedicated to issues of race and culture, Patrisia Macias Rojas and Rebecca Gordon ask, "Is Separate But Equal Really Such a Bad Thing?" They offer the following statistics:

- It's impossible to answer that question, because separate but equal schools do not exist. Schools in this country are both separate and profoundly unequal.
- White suburban schools have vastly more money than inner-city schools, whose students are often 90 to 100 percent children of color. That's because almost half of school funding comes from local property taxes.
- In New York state, the richest school district spent $38,572 per student in 1992. That's seven times what the poorest district spent—$5,423. In Illinois, the ratio was 8 to 1. In Texas, per-student spending ranged from $3,098 to more than 10 times as much—$42,000.

- 92 percent of whites, 86 percent of African Americans, and only 61 percent of Latinos finish high school.
- In metropolitan Philadelphia, inner-city drop-out rates are four times as high as those of suburban schools.
- White high school graduates are much more likely to go to college, and to finish college, than African Americans or Latinos.[5]

Unequal funding lies at the root of many of the problems of public schooling. Lack of materials and training, lack of staff, overcrowding, and crumbling buildings are all results of funding shortages. As long as school funding is linked to property taxes and supplemented by parent donations, schools will continue to be separate and unequal.[6]

Issues of class discrimination invariably accompany issues of economics. In a speech made in Milwaukee, Wisconsin, Ralph Nader stated, "It would be a mistake if we concentrate on just race and not class. They form a mutually reinforcing vicious circle, and although the most emotionally outrageous things come from racial issues, we have to connect them to the larger picture of class issues."[7]

Can You See Me Now?

It is a harried Wednesday morning, two days away from payday. As I am about to walk out of the door, my son reminds me that he's out of lunch money. I check my purse—only a quarter and some pennies. The hour grows later as I check the couch cushions and then my pants pockets, finally putting together the $2.00 that he needs. I include the quarter from my purse.

As I am driving to work that day, I think of the factors that had me searching the cushions of the couch. I am a single parent who does not receive child support. I opted not to take it at the time of my divorce because my wage was much higher then. When I decided that I wanted to explore my talents as an author, I changed jobs and lost about $20,000 of salary per year. Even at that, and couch cushions aside, I feel lucky. I have a stable job as a classroom teacher, a roof overhead, and usually enough money to just get by. More important, I am content with the decisions that I've made thus far. As I pull into the parking lot at work, I give an idle thought to tomorrow's lunch money. I know that I can go to the grocery store tonight and cash a check. I know that it will not clear until Friday. I know that once again, I will get by. But I do take a moment to wonder if the people making the educational policies for my students, many of whom live at extreme poverty levels, have ever had a morning like mine.

We are told, from the time we are little on, that it isn't nice to talk about money. Yet we whisper about Bill's new job or Janice's dream home. We speculate on the wages and expenses of others. We are both annoyed and awed that for some, income is such a non-issue. A few days ago, a teacher friend, Sue, joined a group of us for dinner. She was lamenting a problem with her car, only recently (and finally!) paid off. Another friend asked how bad the damage was, giving us her scale for assessing "bad." She nonchalantly said that if the repair tag was under $1,000, she didn't consider the damage very bad at all. I watched as Sue's eyes teared up. Even the seven-hundred-dollar bill that she faced was more than her financial situation could support. Volunteering that information would have made her feel vastly inferior, so she stayed quiet, managed a smile, and shrugged, stating that she was sure that it would all work out.

I had to type my lunch money story twice. I erased it the first time. Then I debated about whether to include it. There is shame, somehow, in having two master's degrees and yet still be struggling, on occasion, to make ends meet. There has been much written about the invisible poor. Yet, the poor are really not invisible and they are certainly not treated equitably in most public schools. Poverty is not an excuse for not learning, but it is a factor to be considered in learning.

The color lines that continue to separate learners are not invisible, either. Acknowledging them is a first step toward managing an equitable curriculum for all students. Acknowledgment should not be considered a passive write-off of the "way things are" but rather a call toward awareness and action. Journalist Alan Borsuk states, "The urgency of addressing the gap between the accomplishments of minority students and white students in school—and between the economic futures of each—is indisputable. The relationship between education and success has never been greater."[8] The Civil Rights Project at Harvard University echoes this sentiment with some research findings of its own. Black students are classified as needing special education far more often than white students, and are less likely, once they have been identified as having disabilities, to be placed in mainstream classrooms.[9] "It stands to reason that more minorities are in special education because they are poorer," said Jorge E. Amselle, a spokesman for the Center for Equal Opportunity, a Washington-based group that takes a generally conservative stand on racial and ethnic issues in education.[10] According to 1997 data from the U.S. Department of Education, nationally, black students were 2.9 times more likely than whites to be identified as having mental retardation, 1.9 times more likely to be identified with an emotional problem, and 1.3 times more likely to be identified as having a specific learning disability. Researcher Donald Oswald of the Virginia Commonwealth University in Richmond, found that the wealthier a school district, the more likely black males were to be labeled mentally retarded and sent to special classes.[11]

The odds against poor children and children of color are compounded by the fact that as a nation we devote the fewest educational resources to children whose families have the fewest resources.

Amer'ka, "Land of the Free"
Makes a mockery
Of what it means to be
Free

Chaining the poor to car washes
Maid to order

"Do you want fries with that?"
That's right, Blood, you in
Score some ex, take your Baby
For a ride.
From a brown man handcuffed to a taxi.
'Least he has a job.
Yeah, right.

Amer'ka, "Land of the Free"
Makes a mockery
Of what it means to be
Free

Setting the poor in trailer parks
Like puzzle pieces
"It just seems to fit."
Walking away, satisfied.
No lights in the dark (or the day)
No running water
Makes the mac and cheese dry
'Least they got food.
Yeah, right.

Amer'ka, "Land of the Free"
Makes a mockery
Of what it means to be
Free

Telling the children of Goldilocks
While throwing rocks
"Go back to where you came from."
Learn the language, take a bath
Lucky to live in an eroded building
Rats as pets
Just let the landlord touch you
'Least they got freedom.
Yeah, right.

With a bleak picture that has not borne much improvement as we've moved into the twenty-first century, how do school districts begin to address the myriad inequalities faced by students? One group that has chosen to address this topic is the Minority Student Achievement Network (MSAN). MSAN is a national coalition of twenty-one multiracial, urban-suburban school districts across the United States. The Network's mission is to discover, develop, and implement the means to ensure high academic achievement for students of color, specifically African American and Latino students.

Among the core beliefs of MSAN are the following:

- Because achievement is not innately determined, children will achieve when they are effectively taught how to learn.
- All children come to school with a variety of individual strengths; our responsibility as educators is to discover and build upon these strengths.
- Schools that concentrate on how their practices affect students will be more productive than those that blame students, families, or poverty for underachievement.
- Each individual staff member must examine his or her beliefs and change practices to counteract the contemporary and historical impacts of racism and discrimination.
- Schools should be considered excellent only when students of all racial and ethnic groups are achieving at high levels.[12]

There has been an abundance of research in recent years celebrating high-poverty schools that are also evidencing high academic performance. Researcher Douglas Reeves first coined the term "90/90/90" to describe such schools based upon observations in Milwaukee, Wisconsin. These schools were identified as having 90 percent of the students eligible for free and reduced hot lunch, 90 percent of the student body were members of ethnic minority groups, and 90 percent of the students met the district or state academic standard in reading or another area. In studying schools across the United States that met the 90/90/90 criteria, Reeves and his associates determined that there are five attributes common to 90/90/90 schools. These characteristics are:

- A focus on academic achievement
- Clear curriculum choices
- Frequent assessment of student progress and multiple opportunities for improvement
- An emphasis on nonfiction writing
- Collaborative scoring of student work[13]

These traits can serve as the litmus test for all schools, especially those involved in educating learners who have had previously inequitable conditions. Bearing these conditions of learning in mind, the remainder of Chapter 4 will focus on how to increase students' skills in the critical academic areas of reading and language. However, students do not thrive with an academic concentration alone, so Chapter 5 will focus on other educational practices that reflect an exemplary approach to meeting the needs of children.

Let It Be

I've been in the field of education a long time now, and there are a few concepts that I just don't understand. Timed tests, spelling books, and complete sentences are among them. Yet I know that were I to stand up at an assembly of teachers and decry the use of any of these, I might be both heralded and stoned in rapid succession. Just the other day, one of my students was struggling to put his pencil to the paper. I knew that he understood the content. His social studies teacher is thorough and uses multiple modalities to reach her students. I asked him what the struggle was—why he wasn't writing down the answers. He sighed a deep sigh and explained that he had to write out the entirety of the question first, and then write the answer in complete sentences. He'd only recently been released from occupational educational services, had nearly illegible handwriting even when he put effort into it, and, in short, detested the physical act of writing. I told him that I'd help him get started and I wrote the questions for him. Even as I was doing it, I wondered at the educational purpose of recopying a question. My student still wrote his answers in complete sentences (I was not up to a public stoning that day), and he most definitely understood the concepts that the questions from the book were reviewing.

Over the years, one of my teaching philosophies has evolved to Stephen Covey's concept: "Begin with the end in mind."[14] I believe that learning must be adaptive. That is, learning must reflect the individualized needs of students within a classroom. Unfortunately, the standards movement and the shift in focus from students-as-learners to students-as-test-takers dictate that learning be prescriptive. The archaic notion of educational "scope and sequence" has merely been replaced by "standards and benchmarks." There is an explicit expectation that teachers will be able to deliver a cookie-cutter curriculum and produce Stepford children. Policy that slithered its way into becoming legislated mandate tells us that not only can all children learn . . . but that all children *must* learn. And that those children must learn at the same rate as their peers.

Certainly all children can learn. Just as certainly, all children must master the skills of literacy in order to maximize their contributions to our world. Real literacy, however, defies succinct definition. Author Steven Judy writes, "Defining literacy is devilishly difficult," as he cites the differences between functional literacy, "grade level" reading determination, and second graders who can read the fairly sophisticated prose of *Mad* magazine yet struggle with a classroom basal reader. Judy goes on to explain how the concept of literacy has evolved with the mass media explosion of the late twentieth century. The concepts of technological and media-based literacy have come to be widely accepted as part of what a classroom teacher must help her students develop. Judy sums up his thoughts with "Literacy has to do with speaking as well as writing, with theatres as well as libraries, with television as well as novels."[15] It is this definition of literacy that will guide a review of best practice.

I'd like to be able to take a dedicated stance in this section of the book. But the truth of the matter is, I've always been a fence-sitter in the whole language versus phonetic instruction debate. Over the years, I've looked to my students, from prereaders to high school students, to show me the way. All that they've shown me, however, is that each student is unique and thus learns as much through individual development as through instructional design. I'll never forget the day that six-year-old Steven learned to read. It was my second year in education, and for weeks Steven and I had been mercilessly parked in front of kill and drill worksheets, tracing the consonants and practicing the short-vowel sounds. I was sure that one more rat upon a mat would send me careening over the intellectual edge. I was wondering why someone, sometime, in my education courses hadn't told me that reading wasn't prescriptive. Fortunately for Steven (and for me), I had recently attended my first workshop focused on Howard Gardner's theory of multiple intelligences. I knew that Steven was a very physical boy. I'd watched him squirm in his seat, bolt to lunch, skip to physical education class, and nearly fly around the playground at recess. One day, instead of kill and drill, I handed Steven tactile letters. I told him to stand up and hold the "R" over his head and say "Rrrrrrr." When he was done with that, I had him hold the "A" over his round tummy and say the short vowel sound for "a." Then I had him place the "T" at his feet and touch his toes while saying "T-t-t-t-t." After he'd done that a couple times, I put the letters RAT side by side and asked him to tell me the letter sounds. He shifted in his seat, and wiggled his pudgy hands, first toward the ceiling, then toward his tummy, and then toward his toes, saying the sounds in isolation and then proudly combining them into the word "rat." For the first time in my career, I literally saw the light go on in a child's eyes. Soon, Steven was grabbing other letters, going through his calisthenics, and forming new words. Multiple intelligences—one. Kill and drill—zero.

Then there was Chris. Chris was nearing the end of second grade and still not really reading. But Chris could carry on animated discussions about dinosaurs. He pored over picture books of dinosaurs, and told stories of them orally with obvious glee. He seemed to like it when I wrote down his words. Yet he was reticent to read or write them himself. Until the day that I raided the local library for books with fewer pictures. I would sit with Chris and begin to read to him about a tyrannosaurus rex or a brontosaurus. At first, I'd stop only on the obvious words like *dinosaur* and I'd say, "What do you suppose that says?" Chris would give tentative but correct answers. The next time we'd read, I'd say, "Now, we know that you know this word and this word," as I underlined a few words from our previous reading time. I would tell him that those words were his words to read aloud. Soon, I was able to stop at more difficult words and model "sounding them out" for Chris. Later still, I began to encourage Chris to sound out new words for himself. Curiosity and an active interest in dinosaurs led Chris to use what he had already gleaned through the osmosis of two years of phonetic instruction to become a natural reader.

I learned to read at a very early age. I was always a sight word reader with a strong photographic memory that enabled me to learn quickly and with a high degree of retention. I assumed that it would be the same for my son. When I was pregnant with him, I labeled everything in the house with a name. After he was born and began to grow, at his eye level, he was able to see "washer" and "dryer" and "table" and "chair." I eagerly awaited his "revelation of reading." I waited through the ages of three, and four, and five. The labels began to fray and peel and finally fell off each inanimate object, one at a time.

My son is very bright. In fact, he began kindergarten at the age of four. During his kindergarten year, around President's Day, one of the conversations that he initiated began with "Mom, I think that Abraham Lincoln was a lot like a mouse and our country was like an elephant. The country was a little bit afraid of what one person would do." But he still wasn't reading. He wasn't even very interested in letters, save for the messy scrawl that he would devote to his name when he needed to.

At the end of second grade, while on vacation at the beach, he glanced at his stomach and announced that his belly button looked like a bromeliad. I had to ask him what a bromeliad was! However, while he now *could* read (through a laborious process of phonics and memorization), he never *chose* to read. He loved to be read to but he was far too active a child to seek adventure from books. Even when he did sit down to read by himself, he rocked back and forth in a dizzying pattern. I'd often ask if he could really read that way and he'd assure me, "Mom, it's the only way I *can* read."

Today, he is a well-rounded middle schooler with an impressive vocabulary and a mature conversational grace. He can't really spell and still doesn't like to read. Fonts bother him sometimes. Color changes in text disrupt his flow. Photocopies that are of poor quality are a nightmare. He can write good sentences but often the idea of paragraphing totally eludes him. He views PowerPoint, which allows him to segment his thoughts into easily communicated bytes, as a godsend. He'd still rather be up and moving and working with his hands than sitting in even the most comfortable chair at his desk.

The question remains, though, is my son literate? The obvious answer is that of course he is. He has, after all, mastered the "basics" of written language. Yet on a standardized exam in Wisconsin, he may be exactly that—basic. His performance may raise red flags. After all, "basic" can translate into lost funds. Threatened by increasingly punitive measures, districts across the United States are labeling learners like my son as "remedial." They are instilling prescriptive, component instruction to alleviate children's perceived deficits.

As I already mentioned, I'm a fence-sitter. I am not opposed to component instruction *if it works*. And it *does* work for some learners. The vast majority of students that are deemed to be poor readers and writers, however, do not benefit from compartmentalized instruction of isolated skills. Moreover, even when it does work, component instruction implies simple right or wrong answers for every issue that we've got. But how do we discuss major issues in foreign policy, the beauty of a painting, or the problem of nuclear waste? It takes a lot of reading, writing, talking, and listening to address those issues.[16]

Having acknowledged that component instruction does work for some learners, it is now time for me to transition from the fence to the soapbox. Picture having to get an inoculation each morning. You are told that the medicine given is important in preventing a life-threatening disease. So, while it is unpleasant, expensive, and leaves a lingering and distracting ache, you cooperate. Years later, you learn that the injection only works for your colleagues who are male and have red hair. In fact, only those select few are actually at risk of contracting the disease. How do you feel? You've spent years engaged in a painful process that was of little value to you. Perhaps you are simply grateful that you no longer have to face the discomfort each morning. Perhaps you're angry at the wasted time. Still later, you learn that the clinicians who were giving you the shots all those years knew, from the start, that the medicine would only work for a select few. With a simple measure of gender and hair color, you could have been spared years worth of pain. It is then that you become truly angry at the insensitivity of a system that failed to treat you as an individual. Could we possibly be using this unfair system with children?

The use of scope-and-sequence curriculums as yardsticks for measuring all children provides a lucrative market for the publishing industries. Children who do not master skills at the prescribed time and in the prescribed order are considered deficit and in need of remediation. Remediation requires a whole new set of materials and trained personnel. Just as the keepers of the medicine in our mythical example were lining their pockets with the proceeds from those daily injections, so, too, the publishing industry is reaping great profit because insensitive school systems fail to treat students as individuals.

It's ridiculous when you really think about it. We are told that Johnny can't read. But perhaps Johnny simply can't read under the conditions in which he's been taught. Instead of finding a new way to reach Johnny, we heap more of the same on his desk. We purchase more of the same from booksellers. We seem to honestly believe that this will work. Instead, this process is much like speaking louder to a person who speaks a different language. It only serves to make us look foolish.

If It's Broke, You Must Fix It

Before going further, let's set aside the arguments that typically slow educational progress. They are 1) we don't have the time to individualize—our class sizes are huge, 2) I don't have enough books for my classroom—and our library isn't much better, 3) the school district says that I have to be on page 120 by Christmas—when do I have time to be creative?, and 4) I have to teach to the test—keeping my job depends on my students' success with the test.

All of these arguments have validity. However, if we as professionals continue to practice under the belief of any of them, we are doing a great disservice to ourselves, our students, and our communities. In his book *Re-imagine!* Tom Peters offers both a rant and a vision on the subject of education. In his rant, he says, "We attempt to 'reform' an educational system that was designed for the Industrial Age—for a Fordist era where employees needed to 'know their place' and in which employers needed uniformly 'trained' interchangeable 'parts' ('workers' in collars both blue and white). Yet now we must prepare for a world in which value emerges from individual initiative and creativity. And we must reject all notions of 'reform' that merely serve up more of the same: more testing, more 'standards,' more uniformity, more conformity, and more bureaucracy." In his vision, Peters relates, "I imagine a school *system* that recognizes that learning is *natural*, that a love of learning is *normal*, and that real learning is *passionate* learning. I imagine a school *curriculum* that values questions above answers . . . creativity above fact regurgitation . . . individuality above uniformity . . . and excellence above standardized performance. I imagine a *society* that respects its teachers and principals, pays them well, and (most important) grants them the autonomy to do their job . . . as the creative individuals they are, and for the creative individuals in their charge."[17]

It is time for teachers and administrators across the country to be both practical and political. It isn't enough to go to work each day, focused on the students. It isn't enough to close a classroom door and go about the business of education—precisely because education has suddenly become everyone's business. The No Child Left Behind Act has deemed it appropriate that Big Brother step into the classroom, too. But, it doesn't have to be that way. Don't let the arguments against progress become your mantra. Instead, look at states like Maine and New Hampshire that have proposed blocking state funds. Arizona, Hawaii, Minnesota, and New Mexico lawmakers have proposed opt-out measures. So far, lawmakers in twenty states have asked the federal government for changes in the law or for more money. Utah's House Education committee originally approved a measure calling for the state to opt out but later opted only to keep Utah from spending state money on the law. Vermont's Republican governor has signed a similar ban.[18]

Where there is a will, there is a way. Not enough books? Knock on doors, tell the media, and tap into literacy agencies until you get results. When the Edward Williams Elementary school in Mount Vernon, New York, made it clear to the media that their school library was stocked with books from the 1950s and 1960s, a national news article detailing their plight appeared. Now, the school has several large boxes of books waiting to be catalogued and enjoyed.[19]

Consider the World of Opportunity School in Birmingham, Alabama. The World of Opportunity (WOO) opened its doors after the Birmingham city schools pushed out 522 students in an apparent attempt to raise test scores. Steve Orel, WOO coordinator, told the story at Interversity's first online conference, Roots of Resistance, in September 2000. His account of 522 students pushed out of school in Birmingham, Alabama, tells how his objections to the district's actions cost him his job and how the WOO was born. The WOO is a social justice and civil rights experiment that works at teaching the whole person. This means addressing hunger, homelessness, and domestic violence as well as academic needs. Over the past two years the WOO has worked with hundreds of pushed-out students. Nine have passed the GED exam and others are about to take the exam. More than one hundred students have used the WOO's training in computers, health care, and drafting to obtain jobs.[20]

In Colorado, a ten-year-old has taken on the Colorado Student Assessment Program.[21] He will get a zero on the exam and he's sad that this will hurt his school's overall scores. However, he is on a quest for what he called educational justice. Shouldn't the rest of us be, too?

Learning the ABCs

Now that I've made my pitch for *providing literacy programs that are tailored to individual student needs*, I'll offer other basic tenets of reading and writing programs that can be implemented to address the current inequalities among learners. Like Tom Peters, author Stephen Judy believes that literacy instruction cannot be improved without a major overhaul of both its aims and its methods and without a drastic alteration of teaching conditions.[22] I'm inclined to see the picture as slightly less bleak. I believe that there are excellent teachers across the United States who are employing exemplary methods to reach every learner in their classroom. I do not believe that we must reinvent the wheel; rather, we must tap in to the spokes and make certain that they are interconnected. The whole can only be as good as the sum of its parts. In order to individualize instruction, a teacher must know more than one method of teaching. We can learn from one another and we are professionally responsible for doing so.

We are also responsible for meeting the developmental needs of our students. G. Robert Carlsen, a specialist on children's reading, has shown that as children grow, their use and enjoyment of language changes and develops. Stephen Judy adapted his work into five stages:

1. *Unconscious delight* (grades K–6): Engagement with language and literature for the sheer pleasure and satisfaction of a good story, the sounds of words, or the enchantment of the unfamiliar.

2. *Vicarious experience* (grades 6–9): Using language to extend the dimensions of one's universe to learn more about the world and the people who inhabit it.

3. *Seeing oneself* (grades 8–10): Reading and writing used to explore personal experience and to see those experiences in the light of others'.

4. *Expanding consciousness* (grades 10 and up): Language as a means of learning about human issues, problems, and values, and coming to understand the human condition and the perennial questions facing humankind.

5. *Aesthetic Experience* (grades 10 and up): Enjoyment of language and literature because of conscious appreciation of form, structure, and content.[23]

Having worked with middle school students for so many years, I would add just a few things to Judy's list. First, middle schoolers love to read and write about themselves. My students get the most enjoyment out of reading about characters in their own age brackets who share many of the same thoughts and feelings that they themselves are experiencing. The girls like to read about other girls and about their issues with friends and with boys (the romance novel seems to get "younger" every year!) and boys enjoy books in which the hero (a male much like themselves) has a fantastic adventure. It can be a space adventure, a wilderness survival trek, or a medieval romp. It should be noted that any book in which dragons are slain by fierce twelve-year-old warriors will appeal to most middle school boys.

Second, middle school teacher Tanya Lynaugh points out, "If you read it, they will, too" as she describes the solid research basis for not abandoning classroom "read aloud" time when children exit the primary grades. She asserts, "The indisputable truth had been revealed, by those who matter the most, the students. I also learned *reading aloud is not just for elementary classrooms.* Middle school students *do* like to be read to—60 percent of the students surveyed in my middle school said so. In fact, 40 percent stated they wished their teacher would read books aloud more often."[24]

At all stages, reading programs work best when they perform the dual function of stressing independence and recognizing the social values placed on language by society. These two concepts not only assist children with developing a sense of self, but also in placing that self in the context of a global society that increases in scope together with their development. It is also important to recognize that because language and its use are societal issues, success with them can and should be built into all school curricular areas. Literacy is the job of every individual in a school.

A second tactic for uncovering the readers and writers in our classrooms is to *celebrate the buh-buh.* I'll never forget the moment when my nine-month-old son crawled to the coffee table, pulled himself up, and reached for the bottle of juice that was sitting atop the table. Standing tall on his chubby little legs, eyes focused on the prize, he reached. As his fingers wrapped around the bottle, he gave a delighted screech of "Buh-buh!" before plopping back down on the carpet to enjoy his conquest. Clearly, he was communicating. Do you suppose that I sat next to him, held his small face in my hands, and said, "No,

Alexander, that's a bo-ttle. You must say the 't' and the 'l' sound, too." Of course not; I celebrated his attempts at verbalization. After all, isn't the end goal of communication to be understood?

Stephen Judy shares, "Too often teachers approach students' language through grammatical and rhetorical categories that they themselves only came to master late in their academic careers. Thus a statement that seventh graders 'need' work in 'the topic sentence' is little more than imposition of an adult rhetorical concept—the topic sentence—on children who often have no need to write such sentences."[25]

Recently, I required my students to write an "I-search" paper on an issue related to the Holocaust. One of my students bounced into the room, happy to be finished with the typing of her rough draft. When I looked it over, I noticed that she hadn't used the topic sentences that we'd discussed in class. Instead, she had centered all of her text, and proclaimed her subheadings in bright pink font, following them with exclamation points. "What I Already Know!" her paper sang, and her knowledge filled the space below. My first instinct (old habits die hard!) was to draw arrows and indents, to cross off her pink letters, and to fit her paper to the format that we'd discussed. Instead, I asked her why she had chosen this format. "Well, I wanted my paper to be different," she said, "and I chose the pink color because this is such a sad topic I still wanted there to be something cheerful about my paper." Developmentally appropriate reasoning had guided her thoughts. I then asked her if she knew how to write a topic sentence for each paragraph and she assured me that she did. I asked her to do so, aloud, and she told me beautiful topic sentences that could fit each paragraph. Satisfied, I praised her for her creativity and her individuality and allowed her pretty pink letters to continue to sing.

Third, instead of instituting stopgap measures that only Band-Aid the gaping wounds of illiteracy, commit to *stopping the gap* entirely. Stopping the gap requires innovation, not the mindless repetition of what has always been done.

Schools and society say they offer reading instruction as a route to wisdom (and financial success). Yet they have been guilty of using the skill of reading to reinforce the division between the haves and the have-nots, between the literate and the non-literates, between the upper and middle class children (most of whom come from print oriented families) and others (where oral English rather than print receives emphasis). Children from non-print backgrounds are labeled "remedial" and given workbooks and drill, supposedly to correct reading deficiencies. But this kind of treatment has the effect of dooming them to spend the rest of their school lives in non-academic and lower achievement tracks, excluded from courses where upper and middle class students receive their schooling on the way to the university and the good jobs.[26]

Educator James Britton has described language as "the exposed edge of thought."[27] In a study of several communities in one of the Carolinas, Shirley Brice Heath found that children in a black working class neighborhood were treated differently in conversations at home than working-class white children or middle-class children of either race. The working-class black children became competent speakers before they attended school. In her book *Ways with Words,* Heath reports that the black students were more able to play with language, and able to produce rhymes, alliteration, and repetition with ease. But those same children were rarely questioned by adults within their community and virtually never faced the type of "display" questions that are asked in school. Children who appear nonverbal in their early years in school are often quite animated in their homes and communities. They simply don't have the adaptive skills set to evidence their mastery of language in school.[28]

Stephen Judy's criticism of language instruction for minority learners is even more telling. He says,

Although the schools and society have expressed interest in teaching Standard English to all people, they have exhibited considerably more zeal in meting out penalties to speakers of non-standard dialects and creating barriers for them to pass (or trip over). Almost from the day he or she enters school, the non-standard speaker has errors pointed out, "flaws" corrected, his or her "illiteracies" put on display. Since the non-standard speakers are frequently members of minority groups, the emphasis on standard English is used, in effect, to ensure that children of the class in power—the children of white, middle class Americans—will be labeled as "successes" with higher test scores, higher grades, and better job opportunities.[29]

Reading, writing, and speaking are obviously interrelated. I remember my high school chemistry class vividly. It is not a fond memory; I was never able to master the abstract world of molecules and chemical equations. I remember writing my first lab report. Here, at last, was an area where I knew I could excel. Words came naturally to me. My adolescent scrawl filled the page. I had creative ideas that I'd been waiting almost half a year to share! Yet when my instructor called me into his office for a private conference, he was shaking his head. He had my lab report in his hands. "I know that you wrote this," he said, "and I know that you had the best of intentions. I know you wrote it because it is so obviously your voice. It sounds like you. It has an impressive vocabulary and I know that you know the meanings of all the words that you used. If anyone else had used those words, I'd have assumed they were copying it from somewhere. But, you're getting a 'D.' This isn't what a lab report is supposed to be. Look at all these superfluous words! Clear. Concise. Succinct. Say it and be done with it." I left his office convinced that I would never master science or lab reports. It proved to be a self-fulfilling prophecy.

The use of written language in schools naturally parallels the use of oral language. It reveals the same unarticulated attitudes toward children and knowledge; that is, that children don't know much and that knowledge must come to them from on high. Both school talk and fill-in-the-blank exercises and tests also show a preference for certain thought patterns. Most school work requires children to search for one "right" answer, from the teacher or a book, in any given situation.[30] Walt Whitman is quoted as saying, "I have no respect for a man who doesn't know more than one way to spell a word." To begin to bridge the gap of all learners, but especially those in the early grades, teachers must evidence a sincere respect for the language that a child brings to school. More important, the teacher must be able to capitalize on a child's early language experiences and use them as tools to establish well-rounded literacy. Children who are not exposed to books may be less prone to telling stories, but this is not because they don't have stories to tell. Having a variety of print and nonprint resources in a classroom, a consistent time for storytelling (both from adults and children), a means to teach the "conversational basics" that are necessary for school success, access to quality visual media (television programs designed to teach skills, for example), access to appropriate and interactive technology (again, designed to educate), and encouraging children to see themselves as readers and writers from the moment they walk through a classroom door are all conducive to closing the chasm of the background experiences that children possess.

Another critical component in maintaining quality literacy programs, especially as children cross over the education equator in our schools, is to *commit to motivating learners.* Jessie was a thoughtful third grader, hovering near the educational equator. In *Uphill Both Ways*,[31] I define the educational equator as an invisible line of expectation that exists between the primary and the intermediate grades. This imaginary line dictates the supposed "shoulds" that children are simply expected to know as they make the grade-level transition. For example, having crossed the equator, all children *should* know how to raise their hands, *should* sit still, and *should* have all of the supplies needed for class. I was worried that Jessie wouldn't have all the "shoulds." She was the middle child in a large family. There didn't seem to be a great deal of time or money at her house, and the children were frequently left in the ten-year-old's charge while both parents worked. Jessie was distractible and vociferous. That's why I was puzzled one day when the students moved into cooperative circles to construct houses. This type of activity normally appealed to Jessie, yet she sat at her desk with her head down. I walked over to her, asking her what was wrong. She raised her head and looked at me, suddenly seeming far older than her eight years, and as she pushed a straggling long blonde hair out of her deep blue eyes, she sighed and said, "I don't know, Ms. E., some days it's just really hard to get motorvated."

Author Virginia Stuart maintains that

> motivation is the mainspring of the school system. When it isn't wound, all the gears in the system stop and have to be forced into motion. Teachers give students tasks of little apparent purpose or meaning: the students act uninterested. Observing the students' lack of motivation, the teacher may have cynical beliefs confirmed: most children are lazy and don't want to work. In some cases, teachers confuse genuine motivation with "fun" and conclude, like TV programmers, that fun must mean silly, trivial, and gimmicky. Hence, "aids" like Inflatable Mr. P and his friends appear on the scene to entice children to learn their letters. A vicious circle develops when the teacher gets a response to a gimmick and concludes that more are needed.

Stuart also shares the story of third-grade teacher Kathy Diers, who asked her students to copy a poem by Shel Silverstein as part of an exercise focused on handwriting. Diers knew that the poem was comical and anxiously awaited her students' giggles. When none were forthcoming, she asked them why they hadn't found the piece funny. After a long pause, a little boy raised his hand. "Mrs. Diers," he asked, "were we supposed to *read* the poem?"[32]

When it comes to the idea of motivating students, educators, policymakers, legislatures, parents, and communities seem to operate on an educational parallel. That is, that in order to motivate, school systems must take one of two paths. Schools must either "get tough" or "be permissive." Those in the "get tough" camp hail the benefits of a more narrow curriculum—more control of student responses, increased ability to focus on what students "ought" to be learning, and punitive measures that attempt to force students to experience success. On the other side of learning is the "be permissive" sector, using phrases like "at their own rate," "in their own time," "exploratory," and "choice."

Opponents of "get tough" policies point to children frightened into academic submission and sixteen-year-olds still in eighth grade, waiting to pass standardized exams. Adversaries of the "be permissive" approach cite examples of illiterate students who have graduated on the basis of social promotion.

Certainly, none of us wants either outcome for our students. I am puzzled and dismayed at the "either/or" mentality of so many child advocates. Why must a school be tough *or* permissive? Why must there be choice *or* mandate? We are immersed in a society that equates holding students accountable with caring yet refuses to accept that accountability can have implications beyond testing. This same society that envisions a village raising its children does not seem bothered by the fact that the village would rather punish than praise and would rather offer inequity than hope.

As part of his No Child Left Behind plan, George W. Bush has instituted a mandate for an initiative called "Reading First." Within this undertaking, the government provides funding for Direct Instruction (DI) reading programs. In his book, *Reading the Naked Truth: Literacy, Legislation, and Lies,* Gerald Coles provides a thorough analysis of all the scientific studies in the "research base" used to justify the skills-emphasis direct instruction—such as the Open Court program—that is mandated in Bush's "Reading First" legislation. According to Coles, an actual reading of the research shows the following:

- Skills-emphasis direct instruction is not superior to teaching skills as needed. Within a comprehensive, literature-based instructional program, where teachers identify and teach specific skills that children actually need, students learn as well as those taught with a comprehensive, step-by-step program.
- DI is not superior for teaching comprehension. There is little evidence that it benefits comprehension beyond first and second grade.

- DI is not superior to whole language teaching. On conventional reading tests that include tests of skills knowledge, children in whole language classrooms do as well as children taught in DI classrooms.
- DI does not help "at-risk" children. There is little evidence that it helps "disabled" readers overcome their problems and become normal readers.
- **DI is not superior for poor children. There is little evidence that it provides superior reading outcomes for these children.**[33]

Reading First is a phonics-based program that tells teachers what to say. Exactly. It tells them when to say it, and what to write on the board. If this were truly the best way to educate children, couldn't we just skip that fifth year of college that most teachers go through in order to be more knowledgeable about children? Provided that the educators, who most likely never went through a rigorous program like Reading First, actually can still read in spite of their poor childhood training, it really shouldn't take long to teach them how to use the manual. Most of those pesky child development courses could be skipped, too. After all, all we really need to know how to do is to make the children sit down long enough that we can force a single model of reading down their throats, right? And what's next? A model for interpreting art? Poetry? Music programs that forego singing so that children can learn notes? Of course not! There will be no real need for art interpretation in the next fifteen years. Music will all sound the same. When the creativity of teachers is sacrificed for the ideals of a government that is omnipresent but not *actually* present in the classroom, the creativity of future generations is also laid to rest.

George W. Bush's Reading First program, as promulgated by the No Child Left Behind Act, offers the following in its informational materials:

A high-quality, effective reading program must include rigorous assessments with proven validity and reliability. These assessments must measure progress in the five essential components of reading instruction and identify students who may be at risk for reading failure or who are already experiencing reading difficulty. A reading program must include screening assessments, diagnostic assessments and classroom-based instructional assessments of progress. The administration of screening assessments determines which children are at risk for reading difficulty and need additional support. Diagnostic assessments provide more in-depth information on students' skills and instructional needs that forms the basis of the ideal instructional plan. Classroom-based instructional assessments determine whether students are making adequate progress or need more support to achieve grade-level reading outcomes.[34]

When, amid all this testing of five- through eight-year-olds, do you suppose teachers have time to teach? Or to celebrate? Or to make sure that Tosha has breakfast, Gerald gets to his dentist appointment, Jason stops scratching the rash on his face, and Mavis has time to talk about her new puppy?

Consider the words of kindergarten teacher Farin Houk-Cerna, who had been told to sort her students: "I've been told to sort my kids into categories: 'at risk,' 'some risk,' and 'low risk' [of reading failure]. I sit down with my kids and test them: How many letter names can they say in one minute? Disregard any letter that takes them longer than three seconds; it's wrong, and they're off down the road to 'at risk.' How many phonemes (sounds) can they segment in one minute? When I say 'man,' you say /m/ /a/ /n/. Easy! Just make sure that if I say 'trick,' you don't say /tr/ /ick/—that's too many sounds all mushed up together. That might work for real reading, but it won't keep you out of the 'at risk' category!"[35]

My mother must have been an at-risk child. She didn't even go to kindergarten! All I remember about kindergarten is that we played house. Often. I liked to get down on all fours and pretend that I was Barky, the family dog, and while I went to kindergarten already a reader, I don't remember receiving any actual reading instruction. That "tr/ick" question definitely would have bumped me to the risk group.

When my son was in kindergarten, I was most worried that he was going to lose an appendage, even using a safety scissors. He never was one to stay within the lines. Three generations. I guess it's lucky that there's now a program that can solve all of our ills. George Orwell would be proud.

Run, Spot, Run

Richard Meyer, an associate professor at the University of New Mexico, observed, and wrote about in excruciating detail, a phonics lesson that he watched in a primary classroom. Fourteen minutes into the lesson, this is what he observed:

> It's 10:14. Some of the children are watching Karen; others are not. One child has carefully rolled up one leg of his jeans and works at unraveling his sock. He is making a ball with the string of elastic. Since he unweaves only the threads that are parallel to the sole of his foot, he leaves a skeleton of his sock that slips further down his leg as he unwraps further. A few of the children rock back and forth, not paying particular attention to Karen (although it is conjecture to suggest they are not paying attention merely because they are not looking at her). One child quietly makes the sounds of bombs dropping as he moves his hand above the rug and drops it slowly down. One child picks his nose; another plays with her ears; one rubs her hands up and down her braids (later she'll undo and redo them).[36]

In the same lesson, it is always the same one or two students who answer first. Always the same polite children who attempt to pay attention. The only unscripted conversation appears when the children try to make sense of the nonsense words that Karen must create to "expand their phonemic awareness." "Supermad," the children feel, must mean "really angry" and "schoolbun" must be what is wrapped around the hot dogs in the cafeteria.

It is interesting that the children do not pick their noses, talk with one another, and unravel their socks during other parts of their day.

When their teacher reads an actual book to them, they are animated and excited, all of them poised to contribute. When they are released to write in their journals, they do so with relish.

It is much like those inoculations. If you'd ask her, Karen could tell you who the red-headed males are. That is, she could tell you those students that are benefiting from a DI approach. She would also tell you that her classroom was alive with phonics well before the expensive scripted curriculum arrived on her doorstep. But it is likely that Karen won't really tell you any of those things. She has been told by those in power in her district that it is not her job to develop curriculum, it is only her job to deliver it.

All across America, hundreds of children roll up their sleeves, scrunch up their faces, and prepare for their daily hour of pain. For some, the injection is timely and appropriate. For many others, it is simply a progression toward uniformity that will damage their critical thinking skills and their emotional satisfaction with school. Put yourself in their small shoes. In which direction do your feet point? Toward the schoolhouse door? Or decidedly away? Dick and Jane may see Spot run . . . but he is only chasing the children that are running away.

CHAPTER FIVE

Equity Solutions
Within Practice

*Don't worry that children never listen to you. Worry that
they are always watching you.*

— *Robert Fulghum[1]*

Impractical Practice

When I drive past my local hospital, I can't help but feel grateful that
I am alive during the new millennium. I know that the inside of the
building is sterile and white, busy yet efficient, and that the medical
center staff pride themselves on using the most up-to-date, technologically advanced equipment and practices. I could search every
shelf in the hospital and never encounter a medieval jar of leeches even
though medical history would show that the use of leeches dates all
the way back to the very beginnings of civilization.

Leeches have cross-cultural appeal, too. There are documented
records of their widespread use by the Chinese, the Egyptians, and
the Europeans. There are even medically proven facts that support the
use of leeches as treatment for many illnesses. When they attach,
leeches secrete an anesthetic into the skin, allowing blood to keep
flowing painlessly while they feed. There is a chemical in the saliva
of leeches that reduces swelling. And leeches are efficient. Once they
are done feeding, they promptly fall off their hosts.[2]

We've all heard of the skyrocketing costs of health care. Yet none
of us is willing to return to what is no longer best practice in order

to reduce costs. We are not willing to gamble our health on archaic practices because common sense dictates that progress propels improvement.

Why then, do we as an American culture seem so willing to gamble with the education of our children? Why do we so tacitly defer to past practices that perhaps worked once but that are no longer appropriate for children entering a far more technologically advanced world? Putting a new coat of paint on a practice that fell from the educational bandwagon years ago is irresponsible and morally reprehensible. Will Rogers did not go far enough when he said, "If you do what you've always done, you'll get what you've always gotten," because, in fact, if we keep doing what we've historically done in education, we are going to get far less from our learners than in any previous generation.

We cannot keep issuing high-stakes assessments on the coattails of a cookie-cutter curriculum and expect healthy results even though educational history will show that testing dates back to the rudimentary beginnings of schooling.

Testing has cross-cultural appeal, too. Japanese students take tests. So do German students. Students in Bangladesh and Cambodia also take high-pressure exams. At first glance, the tests appear benign. They attach themselves to educational best practice with ease, injecting those that use them with a sense of accomplishment. They provide numbers and data and bar graphs that document specific student achievements (or lack of achievement). And, when the students are sufficiently stressed and enough money has been made, the well-fed test makers quietly pack up their wares for another year and detach themselves from the aching backs of the teachers.

Educational "best practice" has meant many things over the last fifty years. Madeline Hunter's inquiry teaching and Lee Cantor's assertive discipline come to mind. Then there's Howard Gardner's theory of multiple intelligences. And Bill Clinton's Goals 2000. Outcomes-based education. Creative spelling. Heterogeneous grouping. Tracking. Basal readers. Literature circles. New math. There's portfolio assessment, authentic assessment, and performance assessment. And integrated units, thematic units, and multiage grouping. Reading First, Reading Recovery, and being On the Road to Reading. The list goes on and on.

I like some of the things on the list. As you've read this far, you know that there are some elements of the educational bandwagon that I like very much. I like them because I believe that they work. Time and time again the effectiveness of certain strategies has been proven to me and so I highlight those practices above all others when I write. But I wanted this chapter to be different. Issues of equity have never been and can never hope to be solved by Band-Aids or bandwagons.

I worry about the pace of the bandwagons as they come rolling through our schools. They seem to be getting faster each year, with more adept drivers and more clever sayings plastered to the sides of their carriage. In an article for *Phi Delta Kappan,* Professor Maurice Holt discusses the advantages of the "slow school movement." The slow school movement has been borne of an analogy. In 1986, when a McDonald's hamburger franchise opened its doors in the Piazza di Spagna in Rome, a journalist made a joke that turned into a movement. Journalist Carl Petrini quipped, "There's fast food, why not slow food?" and thus the "Slow Food Congress" was hatched into being.[3] Today, in describing themselves, the Slow Food Congress states, "If we wish to enjoy the pleasure which this world can give us, we have to give of our all to strike the right balance of respect and exchange with nature and the environment. This is why we like to define ourselves as 'eco-gastronomes.' The fact is that our pleasure cannot be disconnected from the pleasure of others, but it is likewise connected to the equilibrium we manage to preserve (and in many cases revive) with the environment we live in."[4]

Holt uses the tenets of the slow food movement—philosophical position, tradition, character, the honoring of complexity, and the encouragement of moral choices—as a metaphor for the slow school movement.

"It's reasonable to suppose that Theodore Sizer's Horace would be happy to work in a slow school. The idea that 'less is more' fits exactly with an emphasis on intensive rather than extensive experience. Better to eat one portion of grilled halibut than three king-sized burgers. Better to examine in detail the reasons why Sir Thomas More chose martyrdom or why Alexander Hamilton argued for a strong federal government than to memorize the kings of England or the capitals of the states of the union. The slow school is a place where understanding matters more than coverage; one takes time to see what Newton's concepts of mass and force might imply, to appreciate their abstract nature and the intellectual leap they represent. Then the usual algorithms fall into place quickly and securely. The slow school offers space for scrutiny, argument, and resolution."[5]

In *None of Our Business*,[6] I note that it used to be that the eternal question was, "Which came first, the chicken or the egg?" Our modern results-driven society has formed a new answer to this query. It seems the reply en masse is a chorus of "who cares as long as we have an egg?" Today's students take less time to ponder, less time to process, and move more quickly to producing outcomes than ever before. And who can blame them? We watch fast-paced talk shows, short-lived sitcoms, and music videos that shift our visual focus at astounding rates. Americans eat at fast-food restaurants, invented grocery store express lines, toll-booth pass systems that allow quicker transit, and gas stations, grocery stores, and department stores that encourage consumers to "swipe-and-go." The computer has progressed from dinosaur to Internet road runner, and the plethora of interactive materials that extend reality and shorten attention spans is common everywhere. Students are raised with the belief that faster must be better.

Then we ask them to go back to the basics. Right-wing educational gurus shake their heads and wonder why we can't just return to the good old days of reading, writing, and arithmetic. Policymakers collect standards in cheery baskets and scatter them down the hallways of schools with carefree abandon. Rigor, students are told, is everything. Failing to learn is learning to fail and the only acceptable demonstration of knowledge is the numerical score on a standardized test. Success is not measured in inches. It is not a snapshot of everyday life but a portrait of once-a-year finery. Learning is a product; not a process. It doesn't matter how the answer is found . . . only that it *is* found . . . and, most important, that it can be memorized and transferred to a surreal pencil-and-paper assessment.

Pace and pressure are not unique to the school setting—they are everywhere throughout a child's life. Author Judy Loken refers to it as the "Superkid" phenomenon. A superkid is a hurried child—in every sense of the word: hurried to babysitters, hurried to piano lessons, hurried to gymnastics, hurried to soccer, hurried to dance lessons, hurried to achieve, hurried to grow up. No longer are these childhood years to be frittered away in fun and games. No longer are these impressionable years to be wasted in fantasy and creativity.[7] We do not seem to have the luxury of allowing children to become the learners they want to be, the dreamers they wish to be, nor the expressive thinkers that they ought to be.

Adults face many stresses, too. We are living in pressurized times. Given that problems cannot be solved using the level of thinking that was present when they were created, it seems that the most practical step toward best practice is to *reestablish our sense of perspective.* When did schools become about numbers and dollars instead of about children? When did cheating become a widespread phenomenon instead of a social taboo? Why did negative issues associated with skin color not cease to matter fifty years ago? Why is poverty allowed to hold learning captive? How can we attempt to lead children to the future with a system of carrots and sticks and call ourselves ethical—or call them prepared?

All of these questions can lead to one of two paths—blame or restoration. We've been down the path of blame. It's the policymakers' fault for increasing the pressures. It's the president's fault for passing absurd legislation. It's the community's fault for ignoring the poor. It's the parents' fault for not valuing schools. It's the teachers' fault for not doing more. It's the fault of bigotry, and apathy, and ignorance. The blame game can be played for a very long time, but in the end, it has no winners at all.

In restoration, everyone wins. When students are educated with the skills they need to be productive citizens, there is a nationwide symbiosis. It is written that in 300 B.C., Plato had the following to say on the subject of education: "If you ask what is the good of education in general, the answer is easy: that education makes good men, and good men act nobly."[8] The next obvious question, then, is what is necessary to restore stability to our schools? The foundation upon which schools have been built is solid but the politics and the practice heaped upon that foundation have caused it to wobble. As I looked through all of my notes about best practice, I realized that there was one common theme to the myriad recommended strategies that will allegedly save our schools—all are a reflection of the six character traits of the Character Counts! model[9] that I have been presenting to teachers for use in the classroom for years. It strikes me that these traits extend beyond the doors of the classroom and into the system as a whole. Without them, any measure that is undertaken will only be as good as the wheels on that particular bandwagon. It is for this reason that the remainder of this chapter will look at the traits of trust, respect, responsibility, fairness, caring, and citizenship as they apply to the entirety of our learning organizations.

True-Blue Golden Rules

At the root of all learning and growing are trust and respect. Reciprocal trust and respect among students, parents, and teachers is critical. Trust and respect between teachers, too, is elemental in the progress of a public school. In his 1990 book, *The Fifth Discipline*, Peter Senge pioneered the concept of learning organizations and detailed his vision of the components that are present in such a design. According to Senge, "Learning organizations are organizations where people continually expand their capacity to create the results they truly desire, where new and expansive patterns of thinking are nurtured, where collective aspiration is set free, and where people are continually learning to see the whole together."[10] The rationale behind learning organizations fits in well with both the concepts of "pace" and "restoration." In situations of rapid change, only those that are flexible, adaptive and productive will excel.[11]

Effective learning organizations require systems thinking. However, many school districts, many school buildings, and even many classrooms within a building operate as miniature kingdoms within themselves. Author Margaret Wheatley expresses reservations about whether contemporary K–12 schools can even be called "systems." "The startling conclusion is that most school systems aren't systems. They are only boundary lines drawn by somebody, somewhere. They are not systems because they do not arise from a core of shared beliefs about the purpose of public education. . . . They coexist by defining clear boundaries, creating respectful and disrespectful distances, developing self-protective behaviors, and using power politics to get what they want."[12]

Systems thinking promotes solutions to problems that propel an organization forward. We face small-scale problems every day in the workplace. For the purposes of illustration, I'll use an example of a problem that I've seen solved in two different ways. In the two middle schools that I worked at, teachers were given team planning time as well as an individual preparation period. As it happened, most guest speakers were scheduled during the morning in School A and in the afternoon at School B. At School A, the sixth-grade team of teachers was most affected by the changes in schedule and at School B, it was a team of seventh-grade teachers that was affected. Each time there was a guest speaker, those teachers lost their common as well as their individual planning time. Even though they were not directly responsible for the supervision of students during those times, both the teachers from School A and School B were required to attend the special school assemblies. Both teams of teachers were upset by missing their team and individual planning time.

At first glance, it may seem petty. After all, you may ask, what's a few hours of time? But with five schedule changes a year, those teachers lost a working day's worth of time that their colleagues did not lose. Each team beseeched administration for assistance.

School A had a collaborative building team that met each week. When the team heard the concern, the members devised a schedule wherein they were able to supervise one another's classes on special event days. This exchange of supervision made up for the loss of planning time.

School B's building team chose not to address the need of its seventh-grade team. Resentment built and negative attitudes were visibly apparent. A full one-fifth of teachers at School B were discontented and remained so.

What was the essential difference between the two schools? That can be answered in one word: commitment. School A had made a commitment to adhering to the mission that the entire school staff had developed. They had defined procedures for consensus and systems for responding. Because the school's mission centered on themes of respect, responsibility, and caring, it was only natural that the behaviors of the group also reflect those traits.

Lack of a shared vision is only one stumbling block on the path to continuous improvement. Another stumbling block that authors Hargreaves and Goodson noted is that "the fundamental forms of public education that were designed for an age of heavy manufacturing and mechanical industry are under challenge and fading fast as we move into a world of high technology, flexible workforces, more diverse school populations, downsized administrations and declining resources."[13]

No Small Change

Simply put, change in the education system is imminent. Together, systems thinking and process reengineering ensure that every facet of the school system is focused and aligned toward the mission. Systems thinking implies that someone is giving careful attention to the intricacy of the system, understanding cause and effect. Process reengineering signifies a willingness to improve the system based on that analysis.[14]

It all comes back to the "Plan-Do-Check-Act" (PDCA) cycle described in Chapter 2. However, the *notion* of the PDCA cycle is far different than the *reality* of that cycle. There are many reasons for this. Sometimes, we are just grateful to get a project over with. We are anxious to move on. We convince ourselves that it was "good enough." Typically, however, the "checking and acting" parts of the PDCA cycle get ignored simply because there are so many cycles going on in our lives at one time. It is not as though we are facing only one new practice, intellectual entity, or physical change. Instead, our lives abound with them and they are typically at different phases of the PDCA cycle. Writer Tenneson Woolf adds to this already complex picture with his notion of "living systems."

> Another belief that shapes my perception of learning is "living systems theory," the idea that organizations (and yes, even people) are living systems. Living systems are webs of interaction. Although complex—they continually change, they continually re-create themselves, and they are never wholly predictable—living systems evolve naturally into patterns. Unlike mechanical systems, in which all structure is designed or imposed, living systems organize themselves—they self-organize. And quite remarkably, in people, "meaning" is one of the things that self-organizes. From webs of interacting thought, with self and others, meaning finds a way to order itself. Living systems theory also requires us to re-examine learning—what is learning in a world where order comes freely? What is learning in a world where meaning self-organizes?[15]

Learning in such a world is collaborative. American epigrammist Minna Antrim has said, "To know one's self is wisdom, but to know one's neighbor is genius."[16] A collaborative learning environment encourages people to voice different perspectives, yet an element of risk is present when we unveil our thinking to a group of colleagues. An essential ingredient in collaborative learning environments is an atmosphere of trust. *Trust* in this context refers to the safety level in the group. In a trusting environment, the group is willing to consider the diverse opinions of others. They respect, value, and appreciate the ideas and beliefs of their colleagues. Members are able to speak openly—to express their opinions and beliefs without loss of status or the fear of reprisal.

In a trusting environment, people are safe to say what's on their mind, seek the counsel of others, and experiment with new ideas. This environment offers a place where judgment about spoken communication and actions is suspended. Such an atmosphere invites participation. The following elements are present in environments characterized by high levels of trust:

- *Openness*—inviting all group members to participate by offering information, ideas, thoughts, feelings, and reactions
- *Sharing*—offering materials and resources to help the group move toward its goal
- *Acceptance*—communicating positive regard to other group members about their contributions to the work
- *Support*—recognizing the strengths and capabilities of group members
- *Cooperative intention*—expecting all members to function cooperatively and collaboratively to achieve the group purpose[17]

I remember when one of the school districts that I worked in decided to become collaborative. I thought it was interesting that the mandate for collaboration came solely out of the superintendent's office. I was fairly new to the profession of teaching and always pictured the superintendent's office as an expansive sanctuary locked behind steel doors. My picture may not have been correct but, having never been invited to visit him, I always thought that the superintendent was a bit like the Wizard of Oz. He was the man behind the curtain who had the wisdom to make it all work. So, when the dictum of collaboration was passed down, the junior high where I worked was quick to respond. A site-based, collaborative team was born. I was excited to be a part of this team. In four years, no one had asked my opinion and now I was being given an opportunity to effect necessary change!

Sadly, no changes occurred. My team certainly researched best practice, got the consensus of the staff members who were not on the team, and then recommended proactive changes. The underlings from the superintendent's office told us how valuable our work was, encouraged us to keep working, and denied our requests, reminding us that "the role of the site-based team is merely advisory." There wasn't much enthusiasm on the council after that.

At the start of the next school year, the superintendent was on stage, giving his standard "welcome back" speech. He discussed the "new way of doing things" and mentioned site-based planning and collaboration frequently. Before he finished speaking, though, he requested that the lights be dimmed so that he could show the audience an overhead. On that overhead was the "flow chart" of administrators. His name was poised at the top, followed by that of his assistant superintendents and other central office staff, followed by a listing of all the principals in the district. This, we were told, was the protocol to follow if we had ideas or concerns. In the absence of both trust and respect, true collaboration didn't stand a chance in that school district.

True reform relies on reculturing, not restructuring. Change guru Michael Fullan writes,

> Restructuring is just what it seems to be: changes in the structure, roles, and related formal elements of the organization. The requirement that each school should have a site-based team or a local school coun-

cil is an example of restructuring. If we know anything about restructuring, it is that 1) it is relatively easier to do than reculturing (i.e., restructuring can be legislated) and 2) by itself it makes no difference in the quality of teaching and learning. What does make a difference is reculturing: the process of developing professional learning communities in the school. Reculturing involves going from a situation of limited attention to assessment and pedagogy to a situation in which teachers and others routinely focus on these matters and make associated improvements. Structures can block or facilitate this process, but the development of a professional community must become the key driver of improvement. When this happens, deeper changes in both culture and structure can be accomplished.[18]

Fullan contends that modern schools rely on outside forces such as parent groups, technology, corporate connections, and governmental policy. These external forces, however, do not come in helpful packages; they are an amalgam of complex and uncoordinated phenomena. The work of the school is to figure out how to make its relationship with them a productive one.

He elaborates, "What does the outside look like to schools? Essentially, it is a sea of excessive, inconsistent, relentless demands. Policies are replaced by new ones before they have had a chance to be fully implemented. One policy works at cross-purposes with another one. Above all, the demands of various policies are disjointed. Fragmentation, overload, and incoherence appear to be the natural order."[19]

Collaborative school staffs are able to direct the deluge of outside forces by selecting those that matter most to the school environment. It is akin to choosing "power standards" to teach to students. Staff, too, must have a manageable number of innovations and they must see the relationship between innovation and practice. Organizations must continually examine what they believe and do, seek more information about those beliefs, and then plan for future action. A school environment that encourages individuals to not only contribute to, but also challenge the dynamics of leadership and learning offers the potential for a truly proactive and positive professional environment to flourish.[20]

Almost twenty-five years ago, social change agent Eric Hoffer offered, "In times of drastic change, it is the learners who inherit the future. The learned usually find themselves beautifully equipped to live in a world that no longer exists."[21]

Thus, schools must be learning communities. A learning community, according to superintendent Les Omotani of the Des Moines public schools, is a collection of people who genuinely care about one another, who are committed to strengthening relationships and families through learning and the practice of certain guiding principles, most keyed to questions such as: What are our core values and beliefs? What are we trying to create? How do we honor our children? What matters most of all? Omotani goes on to say, "A learning community is a system whose leaders build the community by nurturing commitment among its members and severely reducing the role of compliance obtained through fear and punishment. Its members make choices and act according to what is in the best interest of the entire system. A learning community is saturated with caring."[22]

Who Cares?

Another aspect of character is evidenced in superintendent Omatani's words—the trait of caring. Sherry Immediato, managing director of the Society for Organizational Learning in Cambridge, Massachusetts, reinforces the notion of building professional learning communities. "Pragmatically speaking," she says, "creating a learning community is a process of asking adults to do what we ask of children. We want adults, from teachers to bus drivers, to focus on critical thinking skills, lifelong learning, teamwork. If you think about it, kids learn more from what they see than from what we say. So if they see adults doing these things, they're more likely to follow suit."[23] Not coincidentally, we also expect our students to demonstrate high levels of caring and respect for their peers. We expect them to be kind when working in groups, to actively listen to one another, and we hope that they will not only tolerate but will appreciate the differences that others have to offer. Why should it be different, then, for any member of a school staff?

In keeping with the theme of equity that this book is devoted to, why should conditions of learning affect a school's ability to operate under the guise of professional learning communities? Realistically, it shouldn't. However, schools that are understaffed, staffed poorly, or that face tremendous budgetary issues will have to be far more determined to enact such a community.

During the 1980s, Susan Rosenholtz brought teachers' workplace factors into the discussion of teaching quality, maintaining that teachers who felt supported in their own ongoing learning and classroom practice were more committed and effective than those who did not receive such confirmation. Support by means of teacher networks, cooperation among colleagues, and expanded professional roles increased teacher efficacy in meeting students' needs. Further, Rosenholtz found that teachers with a high sense of their own efficacy were more likely to adopt new classroom behaviors and also more likely to stay in the profession.[24]

Support and connection foster commitment. Yet good teachers often feel neither. Nationally, the turnover rate for teachers in high-poverty schools is 16 percent, as compared with 9 percent in low-poverty schools. While emergency-certified teachers are more likely to leave the district, attrition among newly certified teachers is substantial as well. Certainly some of these are teachers who determine that they are not cut out for education or leave for more appealing jobs in suburban communities, but the report indicates that this high attrition rate can be attributed largely to dissatisfaction with compensation, working conditions, student discipline, and the leadership in school buildings.[25]

In Philadelphia, approximately 7 percent of the teaching force is brand new in any given year. But due to the centralized hiring and placement process and transfer allowances granted to veteran teachers, new teachers are disproportionately concentrated in high-poverty schools. Again, "the situation is particularly dire at the city's middle schools. It is not uncommon for 20 percent of the staff at the highest-poverty middle schools to have experienced less than a full year of teaching in the district." Since these schools are likely to have the highest number of new teachers, they also tend to have the highest number of emergency-certified teachers.

In addition to suffering inequities in the distribution, new teachers in Philadelphia have another disadvantage: the notoriously late centralized hiring and placement process gives them little time to familiarize themselves with their school, classroom, and neighborhood; meet their colleagues; or plan lessons. Many also reported that there was little in the way of a formal orientation or induction process.[26]

Providing support for new teachers in the forms of mentorships, collegial teams, and helping to make certain that those teachers have both the supplies and the curriculum to conduct business may be costly; but failing to do so has an even greater price. According to a study done by researchers with the Texas Center for Educational Research, teacher turnover costs a district 20 percent of each leaving teacher's annual salary. That means that high-poverty schools are being doubly punished—both by loss of experienced personnel and by the financial ramifications resulting from attrition.[27]

What then, is the harm of enacting a shared vision, promoting team learning, and creating communities of continuous inquiry? Doing so is not only an act of caring for students, but also demonstrates compassion for the complex role of the classroom teacher. Beyond that, though, professional learning communities are more than just congenial opportunities for professional educators to share and develop relationships at work. Certainly, a school atmosphere may exist in which everyone is pleasant. However, this alone does not indicate the existence of a professional learning community (PLC). In a PLC, all individuals within the school setting must value open communication, trust, and continuous inquiry resulting in proactive plans for improvement. Incorporating all dimensions of the PLC (personal mastery, mental models, shared vision, team learning, and systems thinking) is important for student success and school advancement.[28]

Over the years, there have been several definitions of a PLC. DuFour and Eaker broke the phrase into individual terms in an attempt to define a PLC. Thus, a *professional* suggests an individual with expertise in a specialized field, *learning* is an ongoing action and perpetual curiosity, and *community* suggests a systematic arrangement for a definite purpose. They further define a PLC as one where educators create an environment that fosters cooperation, emotional support, and personal growth as they work together to achieve what they cannot accomplish alone. In a PLC, the guiding principles of the vision are "not just articulated by those in positions of leadership, even more important, they are embedded in the hearts and minds of people throughout the school."[29]

The word *community* is very important. Seventh-grade science students in our middle school encounter the word *community* when they learn about plants and animals. Unlike a population, an ecological community is diverse, comprised of several kinds of plants and animals, living in relative harmony with one another. I believe that it should be the same for the school community. To be a true community, we must be more than the people within the walls of our school. There must be a direct and productive outreach to the neighborhoods around our schools, the businesses that help to support our schools, and the social service agencies that interact with the families within our schools. Across America, schools are becoming strongly attached to their communities in innovative and exciting ways, becoming learning communities. Their reasons vary, but include: 1) helping students see links between school and the rest of their lives, 2) increasing parent and community dedication to their schools, 3) improving coordination among schools and other social service agencies, and 4) providing stimulating educational opportunities across the life span. These schools believe that they and their communities can achieve enhanced education for all citizens, both those "inside" and "outside" the school walls.[30] Eric Hoffer's wise words once again come to mind: "The central task of education is to implant a will and facility for learning; it should produce not learned but learning people. The truly human society is a learning society, where grandparents, parents, and children are students together."[31]

The heart of a school-as-learning-community is working together to expand and enrich the learning environment of the school's students. This expanded and enriched milieu uses the intellectual and material resources available in the community as sources for learning. The community is regarded as a many-faceted object of study and one more classroom in which students, collaborating with teachers and other community members, pursue the goals of thinking curricula and assess their progress. In short, the surrounding community becomes a place about which and in which students learn with and from the community's members, organizations, institutions, and businesses.[32]

One such successful community-school model is housed in Chicago, Illinois. The Corporate Community Schools of America is an organization that believes that schools can and must become important centers in children's lives. Children live in families; families live in communities. The texture of family and community life affects the life of a child in school. A school is obligated to do all that it can to help children and their families grow and develop in their personal strengths and competencies as individuals and as members of a community. When families are momentarily or chronically in distress and when their community is also in distress, then the community's key institutions of caring—especially the schools—must go beyond business as usual and find ways of meeting families' needs.[33]

Another good example of a school that cares about its community is the World of Opportunity (WOO) School in Birmingham, Alabama. In *Quashing the Rhetoric of Reform,* authors Eldon Lee and Mary Gale Budzisz describe the WOO. "The school is called the World of Opportunity and is located in a one-floor cinderblock structure with an attached trailer, across the road from a large public-housing project with a primarily African American population on the outskirts of Birmingham . . . As soon as you walk into the WOO, you are struck by the warm glow of humanity that comes from every inch of wall space being covered with pictures of WOO students and messages celebrating their many accomplishments."[34]

Quality schools, whether they are located in the poorest ghettos in the largest cities or in middle America's suburbs, are driven by a commitment to ongoing action. Such schools are restless when they are not engaged in change. However, they are not agents of change for the sake of change, but for continuous progress. Inviting a community into this change can be risky. Unless there is a common language among all participants, change can be seen as chaotic and unnecessary. Offering community education within a public school setting is a good way to not only involve community members in a school but also develop a shared commitment to lifelong learning. Community Education is a philosophy, an expanded view of public education, that learning is lifelong and that self-help efforts foster human dignity, compassion, and individual pride. It advocates a community process through which citizens, schools, government agencies, and community organizations work together to offer education, recreation, and human services to everyone in the community. Community Education promotes:

- Education programs for learners of all ages, backgrounds, and needs
- Full use of school facilities
- Citizen involvement in community problem solving and decision making
- Use of community resources in the kindergarten-through-twelfth-grade curriculum
- Partnerships among community agencies to address community needs.[35]

Community education teaches young children that intellectual curiosity is important and should be satisfied. It teaches adults that they do not need a formal classroom setting or traditional, didactic approaches to learn. It teaches a community that its schools are a resource for all citizens. It teaches the schools that the community is a resource that can be brought into the classroom to enrich the traditional program.[36] What's most appealing about the community education model is that everyone, no matter where their community is located, and no matter their race or income, has something to give.

An Added Responsibility

Responsibility, specifically shared responsibility, is yet another character trait that is infused into best practice. The importance of creating a Professional Learning Community often lies squarely on the shoulders of the school principal to have the necessary knowledge, skills, and resources to create a culture of trust, support, and lifelong learning. It is the responsibility of principals to identify leadership capacity and potential in others.[37] Fullan expands on the importance of this by stating that ultimately, leadership in a culture of change will be judged as effective or ineffective not by who one is as a leader, but by what leadership one produces in others.[38] DuFour and Eaker have three basic questions that drive the work of schools. Answering these three questions on an ongoing basis becomes the responsibility of everyone involved in the school community. The three critical questions are:

- What is it we want to students to learn?
- How will we know they have learned it?
- What are we going to do when we discover that they have not learned it?[39]

Responsible school leaders leave their offices. Often. These leaders spend time in the hallways, in classrooms, and at after-school events. Everywhere they go, they promote the school's mission. They discuss achievement and they model character. The best leaders are successful teachers, working with students directly, modeling best practices for staff, and focusing on the authentic assessment of power standards. Successful principals build relationships and have high expectations. They engage in continuous professional development for themselves and expect their staff to do the same. They provide the materials or funds to support lifelong learning for their staffs.

Principals who thrive demand and cajole continuous progress. In an article on professional learning organizations, Richard DuFour walks his readers through the journey of a successful superintendent. Within DuFour's narrative, a specific five-point plan is provided:

1. Begin with a leadership team. Work with that team to build shared knowledge and a common vocabulary. Take the time necessary to do this step well.

2. Differentiate between consensus and unanimity. Define consensus as "All viewpoints have been heard and the will of the group is evident even to those who must oppose it." Once consensus is achieved, expect appropriate follow-through.

3. Mandate that leaders address the three critical questions on a consistent basis utilizing collaborative teams. Allow flexibility about how results will be monitored and reported among schools.

4. Be certain that all collaborative teams are working toward measurable goals that when accomplished will demonstrate higher levels of student learning.

5. Take time to plan, monitor, model, confront, ask ongoing questions, and to celebrate with all stakeholders.[40]

As I read DuFour's works, I was enlightened by his idea of consensus. When I was a building principal, it was important to me to have staff buy in to any new practices that we were undertaking. Often, I'd introduce the new idea at a staff meeting, simply expecting others to love it as much as I did. More often than not, I was disappointed by a lukewarm reception. Sometimes, I was shocked by an almost hostile response from staff. In his work on organizational leadership, Peter Senge speaks of "differing time horizons."[41] By this he means that goals are often closely linked to roles. As a building principal, I spent much of my time "thinking forward." In my mind, I understood the ultimate goals of the changes that I was proposing. My staff, on the other hand, were often immersed in the immediacy of curriculum delivery and the immensity of student needs. My time horizon may have been five years ahead while a typical teacher's time horizon may have been focused on the next day in school. Obviously, school environments require both types of vision. What's more, progressive atmospheres have the trust, respect, and caring in place so that all participants are able to see the horizons of others.

But let's get back to consensus. Even after I'd learned that I needed to build a common vocabulary and a shared vision before my enthusiasm for a new idea could be contagious, there was always Lou. Lou sat in the back of the library during staff meetings. He did not want to be on our school's building team. He didn't feel pressured to be collaborative. Lou was waiting to retire and wasn't afraid to say so. On the other hand, in the classroom, Lou was a good teacher. He enjoyed the students and they both liked him and learned from him. Whenever a new initiative arose, it pained me to attempt to get consensus from Lou. Eventually, through a "fist to five" process of consensus building, Lou would give a grudging "two" to an idea, mostly so that the meeting would end and he could go home for the day. (In a fist-to-five model of consensus, staff are asked to show support for an idea by giving it a rating of zero [a fist] to five [five fingers]. Those who give ideas a fist or a one must have alternate solutions.) Although good ideas moved forward, his negativity dampened the spirits of the staff. DuFour's model of the "evident will of the group" would have enabled me to capitalize on momentum rather than being waylaid by roadblocks.

Something that I really enjoyed as a principal was starting each day by writing brief notes of appreciation to students, parents, teachers and staff, community members, or to other members of the administrative team. In his research on effective school leaders, Doug Reeves notes that good leaders catch others doing things right. A cardinal principle of leadership, Reeves maintains, is that it is faster and easier to build on strengths than it is to compensate for weaknesses. Leaders must have a daily mission of finding, documenting, celebrating, and replicating effective practice.[42]

Reeves also mentioned that system-level leaders can assist others in maintaining focus by developing "not-to-do" lists. Akin to the narrow (yet critical) focuses of the PLC model, stakeholders are encouraged to eliminate practices that don't service student-centered goals and to be judged on the effective enactment of the goals that do. Some school systems reward school staffs or building principals for successfully meeting the goals that they set for themselves. When one of my school districts did this, I remember having the fleeting notion that I should set goals that were easier to attain instead of those that I'd originally considered. I didn't do so, but can't help but think how much more effective a reward system would be if it celebrated exemplary focus, professional risk taking, and continuous and measurable progress.

It's Not Fair!

One of my major concerns with the No Child Left Behind legislation is that it promotes a myopic view of success. Within a single district, one school may be labeled as a success while another is demoralized by a label of "failing." It does not matter what the demographics of either school is. Focus, risk taking, and continuous progress are bartered for a test score. We tend to think of inner-city children as the most negatively affected by NCLB; however, the president of the Rural School Community Trust, Rachel Tompkins, points out that rural students are affected, too. It seems, then, that the character trait of fairness is at the heart of the issue. Tomkins writes of a case that went before the Arkansas state supreme court. In court testimony, an uncertified high school math teacher working in the Mississipi delta said he is paid $10,000 per year to teach five classes (he makes another $5,000 per year driving the bus). He has two electrical outlets in his classroom, calculators for half the students, and a single blackboard, on which he writes exams by hand because there is no photocopier. He maintained that the expectation of adequate yearly progress was inherently unfair. He won the case.

The federal government cannot substitute pious platitudes about children's being able to learn and accountability for adequate yearly progress for the cold, hard cash schools like Lake View, located in the aforementioned Mississippi Delta, need to buy the services of the good teachers they must have to accomplish these goals. Unfortunately, many rural schools like Lake View will probably never get the chance to see what they can do with adequate and equitable funding. Having starved them of resources for many decades, some policymakers will now blame them for failing to meet high expectations. They will accuse the teachers, leaders, parents, and community of incompetence, neglect, and failure. They will "rescue" these children from their small, close-to-home community schools by closing those schools and busing the pupils somewhere else.[43]

I often tell my students that "fair is what each person needs—and it's up to an adult in your world to help determine needs." This doesn't often satisfy them but with enough relationship building they eventually trust that I am looking out for their best interests. When the secretary of education calls the National Education Association a "terrorist organization"[44] and the president of the United States insists on a system of checks and balances that is highly unbalanced—who is looking out for the teachers? More important, who is looking out for the children?

One of my students has a more direct answer than mine when the cry of "it's not fair" goes up in my classroom. He rolls his eyes, leans in toward the person making the comment, looks them in the eye, and says, "Cry me a river, build me a bridge, and get over it." This doesn't help the perceived victim feel better, either. In fact, it often makes them feel dismissed. It seems to be the answer, though, that our policymakers are asking us to accept. The No Child Left Behind Act is a fine example of "bulldozer legislation." The choices are to get on board the bulldozer, get out of the way, or get run over. Those districts getting out of the way are losing funding. Those getting run over are losing hope.

Statistically, the students being deprived of hope at the most astronomical rates are poor students of color. In and of itself, the lens of class is also crucial in looking at public education. But without the powerful factor of race, that lens is misleading. For example, while many working-class whites attend adequate schools in white suburbs and small towns, the schools attended by working-class students of color are almost universally substandard. Schools where students of color are 90 percent or more of the student body are fourteen times more likely to have a majority of poor students than schools that are overwhelmingly white. Further, almost all rich schools are white schools. Race is a pivotal factor determining the resources available to public schools.[45]

Issues of language, as well as issues of color, trigger the call for fairness in America's public schools. In 1999, California passed Proposition 227, which outlawed bilingual education for California's 1.4 million language minority children. Instead, students are given a one-year window in which to learn English before they are put into mainstream classes. Deborah Ecobedo, an attorney for the rights of the child-learners, maintains that because of Proposition 227, students of color are condemned to a second-class education. Students who cannot get on the "college track" as early as junior high or even elementary school will never catch up to their peers once they enter high school. In reflecting on how parents are treated in this equation, Escobedo says, "I call it the hacienda mentality. They can work in our fields and they can clean our toilets and take care of our children but they're not smart enough to determine what's good for their own children." She views the proposition as an ongoing wake-up call for immigrant parents to educate themselves.[46]

Since the passing of the law, many parents have educated themselves, and an addendum was placed into the law stating that parents could request access to bilingual services. In 2004, 98 percent of such requests were approved. Humanity at last? Well, maybe not. In Santa Rosa, California, a district with a high rate of satisfying the wishes of language-minority parents, a school board member became concerned that too many requests were being honored. Not wishing to invalidate the original proposition (or perhaps simply seeking to not care for children), he drafted a policy that was later put into practice by the district. His policy required parents to show their child is eligible for an alternate program in order to receive a waiver from English instruction. In most cases, a team of the school's educators and the superintendent would have to find that a child has special educational needs. The lack of English fluency alone would not be a basis for an alternate program.[47]

Does this mean that Hispanic parents who only want their children to learn should wish a special education label upon them? That's not only unfair, it's obtuse. I used to read a poem with my middle school students entitled "You'd have to live in someone else's country to understand" and I always wondered—when did America become someone else's country? Has it not always been "ours" and doesn't "ours" indicate a melting pot of possibilities? When we seek first to be understood, before we seek to understand, we do more than harm. We become a danger to ourselves.

What Color Is White?

The man I am dating, who is of both Chinese and Caucasian heritage, has shared with me a story about the cultural sensitivity training that he received while he was in the navy. At the start of the class, the students were told to separate themselves into groups of "black" and "white." He chose to stand with the black students. When questioned on this, his response was that he was neither black nor white and simply didn't really know where to stand.

Racial classifications have long been a means for telling individuals "where to stand." Carol Mukhopadhyay and Rosemary Henze, professors at San Jose University, insist that race, racial classifications, racial stratification, and other forms of racism, including racial ideology, rather than being part of our biology, are part of our culture. Like other cultural forms, both the concept of race and our racial classifications are part of a system we have created. This means that we have the ability to change the system, to transform it, and even to totally eradicate it. Educators, in their role as transmitters of official culture, are particularly well poised to be active change agents in such a transformation.

But how, you may well ask, can teachers or anybody else make people stop classifying by race? And are there any good reasons to do so? These familiar categories—black, white, Asian, Native American, and so on—seem so embedded in U.S. society. They seem so "natural." Of course, that's how culture works. It seems "natural" to think of chicken, but not rats, as food.[48]

We are told that it isn't nice to discuss differences. Many white adolescents feel awkward when issues of race emerge. They are often silent, preferring to say nothing rather than say something insensitive. They are worried that they will sound racist or classist. In a cross-cultural study done with several students from six California high schools, white students reported that they faced ridicule or derision from peers if they displayed ignorance of basic facts about their peers' cultural or racial experience. For instance, one white student said, "I think most black people have made it really evident that you don't say anything slightly racial. When I said once that I didn't know black people get sunburned, I just didn't know. I got totally jumped on." On the other hand, the animosity communicated by students of color is equally understandable, as they have to explain themselves to their white peers while they themselves are immersed in white culture, expectations, and values through the media and the formal curriculum of the school.[49]

Providing safe spaces for students to discuss race is one best practice that all schools should employ. Intentional, thoughtful, guided discussions in which students can explore biases openly will help children to develop a shared vocabulary. Many studies have shown that even very young children are aware of the powerful effects of race in our society or any society. They think about what it means for them to be of African, Asian, European, or Native American ancestry because they need to make sense of their world. They are bombarded with images of race from the news and entertainment media, from their families, from their religious and secular communities, and from their classmates. When teachers avoid the subject, pretending that it doesn't exist as an issue, or when they portray its existence as merely a fringe issue, they send a very strong message. Although this message may be unintentional, the result can be stifling. But when teachers find ways to address the effects of race in society, we have found that children feel liberated. They begin to trust that "the elephant in the room" may be mentioned. And there is more space for them to focus on all kinds of learning.[50]

As I mentioned in Chapter 1, providing a multicultural curriculum is also a best practice response to issues of race. In addition to this, providing training and support for teachers is also critical. Teachers and administrators should have ongoing opportunities to participate in professional development activities that enhance their understanding of racial issues and of the needs of students who engage in dialogues on race. Addressing issues students raise in the context of classroom discussions, especially when they are contentious, is very difficult. This is true for white teachers, who, like many of their white students, may have limited experience talking explicitly about race. It is also true, however, for teachers of color, who are often disproportionately responsible for teaching a diversity-based curriculum. These teachers could benefit from exposure to techniques for responding to the attitudes and perspectives communicated by white students in a way that will challenge their thinking without alienating them from the dialogue.

Similarly, teachers responsible for core courses would benefit from ongoing training on how to further integrate diversity and antiracist topics into their classroom curricula. White teachers need to model risk taking by admitting that they don't have the solutions to race problems, but they also need to fulfill their social responsibility to support young people as they learn to thoughtfully consider these difficult issues. Multiracial schools face enormous challenges in addressing the wide array of needs that their students present.[51]

In the Next Fifty Years

There is a perilous cost of not discussing issues of inequity. There is also a perilous cost in only *discussing* issues of race, poverty, and learning style. That is, if we content ourselves with words instead of actions, we cannot achieve real goals. I'm sure that most of you have had students standing at your desk, red-faced, practically shouting those famous last words, "But I know I handed it in!" You might sigh in frustration, nod with forbearing patience, or gesture disapprovingly at the stack of work on your desk. Neither your response nor your student's assertion can make the paper appear.

More often than not, your student's conviction is real. They are certain that you've lost their hard work. They remember doing it and because they did it; they remember handing it in. More often than not, too, the wayward assignment is wedged into the bottom of the student's locker. Why, then, is there such an ongoing disparity between perception and reality?

There are no easy answers but a likely explanation is that our minds play realistic tricks on us. Sometimes, when we complete an activity, our consciousness renders it "finished" and sends it into our subconscious. Thus, when we later reflect on the activity, we are convinced that all loose ends are tidied. After all, our conscious mind has already relegated the activity to "history" rather than "present."

As I am preparing to tidy the very tangled threads of the inequities that our students face, I am struck by the notion that we, as adults, are behaving somewhat like our red-faced students. When we give to a charity (or two or three or four), our part in redressing poverty is "finished." When we modify an assignment or two, our outreach to children with nontraditional learning styles is "finished." When we remember to speak about the heroes of our students, be they black or Hispanic or Laotian, we are "finished."

I realize that this is a simplistic analogy. We who care about kids—who really care—are rarely satisfied with single measures of reform. Yet consider the words of author Pedro Naguera: "The de facto segregation of so many of our nation's schools is no longer an issue that generates conflict and controversy. Like the growing prison population and homelessness, racial segregation is accepted as a permanent feature of life in America. Across the country, schools are segregated in terms of race and class, and as was true before *Brown*, the vast majority of poor children are relegated to an inferior education."[52]

It has been fifty years since the famous *Brown v. Board of Education* decision that mandated desegregation. Is it possible that the banging of the gavel was the signal for too many that the struggle was "finished"? Certainly not for too many African Americans—not in 1954 and not today. Ironically, passive indifference has succeeded where massive resistance failed. The orders of desegregation have not created an imperative for integration. To the contrary, the high court has rendered judgments since *Brown* that ensure its ineffectiveness. The court has, for example, endorsed racial divisions if they coincide with city-suburb boundaries, and has accepted racial patterns that emerge from housing choices.[53]

Could it be, too, that we once developed curriculum binders, placed them upon shelves, and watched them gather dust—because our efforts were finished? Georgia State University professor Asa Hilliard III affirms, "In the absence of a real understanding of the structure of domination, some of the worst elements of segregation have returned, in new guises. Tracking is less visible, but it persists. Today's scripted, standardized, cookie-cutter, minimum-competency managed instruction, sometimes by private contractors, with severely reduced parent and community involvement, is offered mainly in low-income minority cultural group schools. Affluent public or private schools rarely if ever use the scripted, non-intellectual robotic programs. This is the new segregation."[54] Jonathan Kozol echoes this sentiment with strong words of his own:

> The punitive testing and accountability agendas set in place in the past decade have not lessened these divisions and, indeed, have deepened them by forcing many inner-city schools to gravitate to drill-and-grill curriculums, keyed tightly to the isolated particles of knowledge to be tested by exams, which leave no room for the more wholesome and authentic forms of learning that cannot be measured by empirical assessments. Critical consciousness in schools like these has been subordinated to the goal of turning children of minorities into examination soldiers—unquestioning and docile followers of proto-military regulations.
>
> This is only one of several areas in which young activists ought to be challenging their elders. They should be mobilizing, too, against the mania of high-stakes testing and the associated policies of nonpromotion and nongraduation that are driving an increasing number of black and Latino students to drop out of high school altogether. They ought to be demanding that the political candidates speak out forthrightly on these issues. Instead of pressing the candidates merely to modify the more draconian aspects of "No Child Left Behind," they ought to be asking why this simple-minded and destructive legacy of President Bush ought not to be overthrown in its entirety. Hard issues need hard questions.[55]

Hard issues also need to be made public. Writer Mari Matsuda calls for witnesses. Without witnesses, without the influence and entitlement that educated parents bring, it is hard to muster the political will to provide the simple things we need to fix our public schools: well-maintained buildings; a textbook for every child; well-trained and well-paid teachers; small classes; wrap-around social services; rich curriculum that includes the art, music, and sports that we cut long ago; early intervention for the at-risk; and enrichment programs to retain the privileged and their much-needed social capital. It is no mystery. The privatizers have hoodwinked us into believing that public education, like poverty, is hopeless.[56]

The good news is that our situation is far from hopeless. After all, the assignment is in the bottom of the locker. There is time to act, a will to act, and a means to act. We have the resources to enact best practices, the technology to make our country more cohesive instead of more divisive, and the intelligence to engage in revolt, reform, and resolution. Best practice begins with the reflection that we see in our mirrors each morning, and we need only to look into the eyes of the children to realize that we are not "finished."

We hold the hope of children in our hearts and in our hands. Every journey begins with a single step. Before you close this book and put it on the shelf because it's "finished," make a plan to take one step on your journey. Write it down, tell a friend, and then begin to march. It is a long road to equality. I wish you Godspeed.

Notes

Introduction

1. Gordon, E. 1999. *Education and Justice: A View from the Back of the Bus.* New York: Teachers College Press, 46.
2. Sennett, R. 2003. *Respect in a World of Inequality.* New York: W.W. Norton, Introduction.

Chapter 1

1. Kozol, J. 1975. *The Night is Dark and I am Far from Home.* Boston: Houghton Mifflin, 105.
2. *The American Heritage Dictionary,* 4th ed., s.v. "equity."
3. Nieto, S. 1999. *Affirming Diversity.* Boston: Addison-Wesley.
4. Reinhard, B. 1998. "One Size Fits All." *Education Week* 17, no. 17 (January 8): 109–15.
5. Nieto, 1995. See note 3.
6. Tapia, R., and C. Lanius. 2000. "Underrepresented Minority Achievement and Course Taking—The Kindergarten Graduate Continuum." Presented at NISE Forum: Diversity and Equity Issues in Mathematics and Science Education, Detroit, MI, May 22–23.
7. "Race: The Power of Illusion." 2003. Press Release. January 29. Independent Television Service: San Francisco, CA.
8. Tapia and Lanius. 2000: 4. See Note 6.
9. "Community Correlates of Rural Youth Violence." OJJDP Bulletin. May 2003. Washington, D.C.: Office of Juvenile Justice and Delinquency Prevention.
10. Tapia and Lanius. 2000. See note 6.

11. Reinhard. 1998. See note 4.
12. Flores, B., P. Cousin, and E. Diaz. 1998. "Transforming Deficit Myths about Learning, Language, and Culture." *Literacy Instruction for Culturally and Linguistically Diverse Students,* ed. M. F. Opitz. Newark, DE. International Reading Association.
13. Nieto. 1999. See note 3.
14. Kozol. 1975. See note 1.
15. Straw, D. 2003. "An Era of Change." *Black Issues in Higher Education* 20, no. 9 (June 19): 36.
16. Landsman, J. 2001. *A White Teacher Talks about Race.* Lanham, MD: Rowman and Littlefield Publishing.
17. Sennett, R. 2003. *Respect in a World of Inequality.* New York: W.W. Norton, 54.
18. Nieto. 1999. See note 3.
19. Sennett. 2003. See note 17.
20. Nieto. 1999. See note 3.
21. Landsman. 2001: 5. See note 16.
22. Kozol. 1975. See note 1.
23. Nieto. 1999. See note 3.
24. Nieto. 1999. See note 3.
25. Kozol, J. 1996. *Amazing Grace.* New York: Perennial.
26. Mills, K. 1999. *Something Better for My Children: The History of Head Start.* New York: Plume.
27. Kozol. 1996: 114. See note 25.
28. Gordon, E. 1999. *Education and Justice: A View from the Back of the Bus.* New York: Teachers College Press.
29. "A Portrait of Poverty in Oregon." Oregon State University Extension Service. Cited 21 September 2003. Available from: *http://eesc.orst.edu/agcomwebfile/edmat/html/em/em8743/part3/minorities.html*
30. Reinhard. 1998: 110. See note 4.
31. Kozol. 1996. See note 27.
32. Nieto. 1999. See note 3.
33. Landsman. 2001: 152. See note 16.
34. Kozol. 1975: 7. See note 1.
35. Kozol. 1996. See note 27.

36. Gatto, J. 1991. *Dumbing Us Down: The Hidden Curriculum of Compulsory Schooling.* Gabriola Island, BC: New Society.
37. Kozol. 1975: 24. See note 1.
38. Davis, E. (ed), J. Martin, R. Holcomb, L. and Fisher. 1998. *The Slick Boys: A Ten-Point Plan to Rescue Your Community by Three Chicago Cops Who Are Making It Happen.* New York: Simon and Schuster, 23–26.
39. "Here's to the Crazy Ones." Apple Corporation. Cited 1 September 2003. Available from: *http://www.apple.com/thinkdifferent/*.
40. Hartmann. T. 1997. *Attention Deficit Disorder: A Different Perception.* Grass Valley, CA: Underwood.
41. Pilkey, D. 1999. *Captain Underpants and the Attack of the Talking Toilets.* New York: Scholastic, 141.
42. Pilkey, D. 1997. *The Adventures of Captain Underpants.* New York: Scholastic, 123.
43. England, C. 2004. *Uphill Both Ways: Helping Students Who Struggle in School.* Portsmouth, NH: Heinemann.
44. Levine, M. 2003. *A Mind at a Time.* New York: Simon and Schuster.
45. Armstrong, T. 1997. *In Their Own Way.* New York: J. P. Tarcher.
46. Nieto. 1999. See note 3.
47. Sizer, T., and N. Sizer. 2000. *The Students Are Watching: Schools and the Moral Contract.* Boston: Beacon Press.

Chapter 2

1. "Quote Unquote." Character Counts! Coalition. Cited 1 October 2003. Available from: *http://www.josephsoninstitute.org/quotes/quote-fairness.htm*.
2. Walker, S. 2000. "Assessment—High Stakes Testing/Competency." *State Education Leader.* 18, No. 1 (Winter).
3. *A Nation at Risk.* 1983. National Commission on Excellence in Education. Washington, D.C.: The Commission.
4. Phillips, S. E. 1993. *Legal Implications of High-Stakes Assessment: What States Should Know.* Oak Brook, IL: North Central Regional Educational Laboratory.

5. Hoover, R., and K. Shook. 2003. "School Reform and Accountability: Some Implications and Issues for Democracy and Fair Play." *Democracy & Education*. 14, no. 4: 81.

6. Hoover and Shook. 2003. See note 5.

7. Kozol, J. 1996. *Amazing Grace*. New York: Perennial, 42.

8. Cooney, Fr. Greg. 2001. "The Social Conscience of Vincent de Paul." *Oceania Vincentian*. Australian Province of the Vincentians. Cited 1 November 2003. Available from: *http://www.vincentians.org.au/vinstudiesconsc.htm.*

9. Ryman, A., and O. Madrid. 2004. "Hispanics Upset By Teacher's Discipline." *The Arizona Republic*. January 17.

10. Metcalf, S. 2002. "Reading Between the Lines." *The Nation*. Posted January 10, 2002, at *http://www.thenation.com/doc.mhtml?i20020128&s=metcalf.*

11. England, C. 2004. *Uphill Both Ways: Helping Students Who Struggle in School*. Portsmouth, NH: Heinemann.

12. Dumas, Alexandre. 1981. *Count of Monte Cristo*. New York: Bantam Books.

13. U.S. Department of Education. 1998. *Toolkit98*. Northwest Regional Educational Laboratory U.S. Dept. of Education, Office of Educational Research and Improvement, Educational Resources Information Center.

14. Sacks, P. 2001. *Standardized Minds: The High Price of America's Testing Culture and What We Can Do to Change It*. New York: Perseus Books.

15. Metcalf. 2002. See note 10.

16. Metcalf. 2002. See note 10.

17. England, C. 2003. *None of Our Business: Why Business Models Don't Work in Schools*. Portsmouth, NH: Heinemann.

18. England. 2004. See note 11.

19. Reeves, D. 2001. "Putting It All Together—Classroom Assessment—The Key to Improved Student Achievement. Part 2 of a Series." *Focus on Achievement* 3, no. 1 (November).

20. "The Value of Formative Assessment." 1999. *FairTest Examiner*. Winter. Cited on 9 January 2004. Available from: *http://www.fairtest.org/examarts/winter99/k-forma3.html.*

21. Black, P., and D. William. 1998. "Inside the Black Box: Raising Standards Through Classroom Assessment." *Phi Delta Kappan* 80, no. 2 (October): 139–144, 146–148.

22. *FairTest Examiner*. 1999. See note 20.

23. Black and William. 1998. See note 21.

24. Marzano, R., and D. Pickering. 1992. *Dimensions of Learning*. Alexandria, VA: Association for Supervision and Curriculum Development.

25. Black and William. 1998. See note 21.

26. Darling-Hammond, L. 1994. "Performance-Based Assessment and Educational Equity." *Harvard Educational Review* 64, no. 1: 5–30.

27. Lam, T. 1995. "Fairness in Performance Assessment." Online. ERIC Clearinghouse on Counseling and Student Services. Cited 9 January 2004. ERIC Identifier: ED391982.

Chapter 3

1. "Creative Quotations." Standards. Cited 15 March 2004. Available from: *http://www.creativequotations.com/one/451b.htm*.

2. Gratz, D. 2003. "Leaving No Child Behind." *Education Week*. June 11.

3. Hardy, L. 2000. "The Trouble with Standards." *American School Board Journal*. September. Available from: *http://www.asbj.com/200010910900coverstory.html*.

4. "Why Standards? Equity for All Students." Cited 29 March 2004. Available from: *http://www.achieve.org/achieve.nsf/WhyStandards_Equity?open*.

5. Ainsworth, L. 2003. "Power Standards." Indiana Computer Educators' Conference. January 24. Indianapolis, IN.

6. Madaus, G. 1994. "A Technological and Historic Consideration of Equity Issues Associated with Proposals to Change the Nation's Testing Policy. *Harvard Educational Review* 1, no. 64: 87.

7. Apple, M. W. 1992. "Do the Standards Go Far Enough? Power, Policy, and Practice in Mathematics Education." *Journal for Research in Mathematics Education,* 23, no. 5: 412–431.

8. Gratz. 2003. See Note 2.

9. Ibid.

10. Barndt, M., and J. McNally. 2001. "Nicolet vs. Custer: How Unequal School Funding Affects Education." *The Return to Separate and Unequal: Metropolitan Milwaukee School Funding Through a Racial Lens.* A Rethinking Schools Report. Cited 15 March 2004. Available from: *http://www.rethinkingschools.com.*

11. Moore, G. 2001. "Securing Our Future: Eliminating Wisconsin's Educational Disparity." *The Return to Separate and Unequal: Metropolitan Milwaukee School Funding Through a Racial Lens.* A Rethinking Schools Report. Cited 15 March 2004. Available from: *http://www.rethinkingschools.com.*

12. This research is analyzed in School Communities That Work, *First Steps to a Level Playing Field.* 2002. Providence: Annenberg Institute for School Reform, Brown University.

13. Allgood, W., and R. Rothstein. 2001. "Beyond Equity to Adequacy: Students in Urban Districts Need More Money Than Suburban Schools." *The Return to Separate and Unequal: Metropolitan Milwaukee School Funding Through a Racial Lens.* A Rethinking Schools Report. Cited 15 March 2004. Available from: *http://www.rethinkingschools.com.*

14. Beam, J. 2002. "Towards Education Justice." *Education Week.* September 25.

15. England, C. 2004. *Uphill Both Ways: Helping Students Who Struggle in School.* Portsmouth, NH: Heinemann.

16. American Library Association. "Information Power: Building Partnerships for Learning." Cited 5 April 2004. Available from: *http://www.ala.org/ala/aasl/aaslproftools/informationpower/information-literacy.htm*

17. Ainsworth. 2003. See note 5.

18. Suess, Dr. 1976. *The Sneetches and Other Stories.* New York: Random House.

19. Gatto, J. 2002. *A Different Kind of Teacher: Solving the Crisis of American Schooling.* Berkeley, CA: Berkeley Hills Books.

20. Gates, F. 1913. Occasional Paper #1, *The Country School of Tomorrow.* New York: General Education Board (Rockefeller

Foundation). Note: Also published in August 1912 edition of periodical: *The World's Work*, under same article title.

21. Peters, T. 2003. *Re-imagine! Business Excellence in a Disruptive Age.* London: Dorling Kindersley, 290.

22. Kozol, J. 1996. *Amazing Grace.* New York: Perennial, 31.

Chapter 4

1. Cited 27 January 2004. Available from: *http://www.giga-usa.com/gigaweb1/quotes2/qutopheroesx001.htm*

2. England, C. 2004. *Uphill Both Ways: Helping Students Who Struggle in School.* Portsmouth, NH: Heinemann.

3. Piana, L. 1999. "Reading, Writing, Race, and Resegregation: 45 Years After *Brown v. Board of Education.*" *ColorLines* 2, no. 1 (Spring).

4. Rojas, P., and R. Gordon. 1999. "Just Facts: Racial Resegregation and Inequality in the Public Schools." *ColorLines* 2, no. 1 (Spring).

5. Ibid. See note 4.

6. Piana. 1999. See note 3.

7. Malveaux, J. 2002. "Class Matters for Economic Prosperity." *Black Issues for Higher Education.* July 4.

8. Borsuk, A. 2004. "Dream of Equal Schooling Is Unrealized." *Milwaukee Journal-Sentinel.* January 3. Original URL: *http://www.jsonline.com/news/metro/jan04/197222.asp.*

9. Civil Rights Project. 2002. "Racial Inequity in Special Education: Executive Summary for Federal Policy Makers." Cited 7 May 2004. Available from: *http://www.civilrightsproject.harvard.edu/.*

10. Fine, L. 2001. "Studies Examine Racial Disparities in Special Education." *Education Week.* March 14: 6.

11. Borsuk. 2004. See note 8.

12. Lewis, A. 2003. "A Continuing American Dilemma." ." *Phi Delta Kappan* 85, no. 4 (October): 259–60. Additional information about MSAN can be found at http://www.msanetwork.org.

13. Reeves, D. 2000. *Accountability in Action: A Blueprint for Learning.* St. Petersburg, FL: Advanced Learning Centers.

14. Covey, S. 1990. *Seven Habits of Highly Effective People.* New York: Simon & Schuster, 95.

15. Judy, S. 1980. *The ABCs of Literacy: A Guide for Parents and Educators.* New York: Oxford University Press.

16. Graves, D., and V. Stuart. 1985. *Write from the Start: Tapping Your Child's Natural Writing Ability.* New York: E. P. Dutton.

17. Peters, T. 2003. *Re-imagine! Business Excellence in a Disruptive Age.* London: Dorling Kindersley, Introduction.

18. Toppo, G. 2004. "States fight No Child Left Behind, Calling It Intrusive." *USA Today.* February 11.

19. Wilson, D. M. 2004. "Books Pour into Williams Elementary School." Cited 7 May 2004. Available from: *http://www.thejournal-news.com/newsroom/032304/b01p23library.html.*

20. Information available at *http://www.worldofopportunitywoo.org.*

21. Rodriguez, C. 2004. "A Ten-year-old Goes to Battle Against CSAP." *Denver Post.* March 15.

22. Judy, 1980. See note 15.

23. Carlsen, G. 1974. "Literature Is." *English Journal* 63: 23–27.

24. Lynaugh, T. 2004. "If You Read It, They Will, Too!" *WAMLE Journal.* Spring, 18.

25. Judy. 1980. See note 15.

26. Ibid.

27. Fillion, B. 1983. "Let Me See You Learn." *Language Arts.* September.

28. Heath, S. 1983. *Ways with Words: Ethnography of Communication, Communities, and Classrooms.* Cambridge, UK: Cambridge University Press.

29. Judy. 1980. See note 15.

30. Graves and Stuart. 1985. See note 16.

31. England. 2004. See note 2.

32. Graves and Stuart. 1985. See note 16.

33. Coles, G. 2003. *Reading the Naked Truth: Literacy, Legislation, and Lies.* Portsmouth, NH: Heinemann.

34. Commonwealth of Virginia. "Reading First Overview and Guidance." Cited 7 May 2004. Available from: *http://www.pen.k12.va.us/VDOE/Instruction/Reading/ReadingFirstOverviewandGuidance.pdf.*

35. Houk-Cerna, F. 2003. "Society's Failures Raise Child's Risk of Reading Failure." *The (Tacoma) News Tribune.* Cited 30 January 2004. Original source: http://www.tribnet.com. Available at: http://groups.yahoo.com/group/ACTNOW2003/message/1825.

36. Meyer, R. 2003. "Captives of the Script: Killing Us Softly with Phonics." *Rethinking Schools Online* 17, no. 4 (Summer). Available from: http://www.rethinkingschools.org/special-reports/bushplan/capt174.shtml.

Chapter 5

1. "Quote Unquote." Character Counts! Coalition. Cited 1 May 2004. Available from: *http://www.josephsoninstitute.org/quotes/quoteeducation.htm.*

2. Sohn, M. 1997. "Leeches: Medicine of Old?" *Bookmark: A Publication of the Robert W. Woodruff Health Science Center Library.* November.

3. Holt, M. 2002. "It's Time to Start the Slow School Movement." *Phi Delta Kappan* 84, no. 4 (December): 265–71.

4. "All About Slow Food." Cited 19 April 2004. Available from: *http://www.slowfood.com/eng/sf_cose/sf_cose.lasso.*

5. Holt. 2002. See note 3.

6. England, C. 2003. *None of Our Business: Why Business Models Don't Work in Schools.* Portsmouth, NH: Heinemann Publishing.

7. Loken, J. *Teacher, I Can't Learn School.* Available from: *http://www.northernlightsdesign.com/teacher/#anchor1291855.*

8. Plato. See note 1.

9. Further information available at www.charactercounts.org.

10. Senge, P. 1990. *The Fifth Discipline.* London: Random House.

11. Smith, M. 2001. "Peter Senge and the Learning Organization." *The Encyclopedia of Informal Education.* Cited 9 January 2004. Available from: *http://www.infed.org/thinkers/senge.htm.*

12. Wheatley, M. 1999. "Bringing Schools Back to Life: Schools as Living Systems" in *Creating Successful School Systems: Voices from the University, the Field, and the Community.* Norwood, MA: Christopher Gordon. See also *www.margaretwheatley.com/articles/lifetoschools.html.*

13. Hargreaves, A., and I. Goodson.1999. Series editor preface. In *Changing Leadership for Changing Times,* ed. K. Leithwood (first, unnumbered page). Buckingham, UK: Open University Press.
14. North Central Regional Education Laboratory. "Indicator: Systems Thinking and Process Reengineering." Cited 7 May 2004. Available from: *http://www.ncrel.org/engauge/framewk/sys/think/systhin.htm*
15. Woolf, T. "What Is Learning? It Depends on Beliefs, of Course." *WHOLE.* September. Source: *http://www.whole.org.*
16. "Quotes on Personal Characteristics." Cited 17 May 2004. Available from: *http://writeonill.org/personal_characteristics.htm.*
17. Ward, P., and M. Castleberry. (eds). 2000. *Educators as Learners: Creating a Professional Learning Community in Your School.* Alexandria, VA: Association for Supervision and Curriculum Development.
18. Fullan, M. 2000. "The Three Stories of Education Reform." *Phi Delta Kappan* 81, no. 8 (April): 581–84.
19. Ibid.
20. Gies, L. 2004. "Examining Staff Perceptions Regarding the Existence of a Professional Learning Community at the Middle School Level. Final paper for the Ed 741 Applied Research: Leadership Practicum. Cardinal Stritch College, Milwaukee, WI.
21. Small Business Notes. "Quotations Beginning with the Letter I." Cited 17 May 2004. Available from: *www.smallbusinessnotes.com/history/quotations/alphabetical/i.html.*
22. LaFee, S. 2003. "Professional Learning Communities." *The School Administrator.* May. Available from: *http://www.aasa.org/publications/sa/2003_05/LaFee.htm*
23. Ibid.
24. Rosenholtz, S. 1989. *Teacher's Workplace: The Social Organization of Schools.* New York: Longman.
25. Schmitt, L. "Philadelphia Faces the Challenge: A Qualified Teacher in Every Classroom." Cited 14 May 2004. Available from: *http://www.gse.upenn.edu/review/article_3.html.*
26. Ibid.
27. Benner, A. 2000. "The Cost of Teacher Turnover." Austin, TX: Texas Center for Educational Research.

28. Gies. 2004. See note 20.

29. DuFour, R., and R. Eaker. 1998. *Professional Learning Communities at Work.* Bloomington, IN: National Education Service.

30. Tinzmann, M., L. Friedman, S. Jewell-Kelly, P. Mootry, P. Nachtigal and C. Fine. 1990. "Why Should Schools Be Learning Communities?" Oak Brook, IL: North Central Regional Education Laboratory.

31. The Eric Hoffer Resource. Cited 14 May 2004. Available from: *http://www.erichoffer.net/quotes.html.*

32. Tinzmann, et al. 1990. See note 30.

33. Ibid.

34. Lee, E., and M. Budzisz. 2004. *Quashing the Rhetoric of Reform: An Educational Design that Reaches All Children.* Lanham, MD: Scarecrow Publishing, 148.

35. See note 30.

36. Tinzmann, et al. 1990. See note 30.

37. Danielson, C. 2002. *Enhancing Student Achievement: A Framework for School Improvement.* Alexandria, VA: Association for Supervision and Curriculum Development.

38. Fullan, M. 2002. *Leadership in a Culture of Change.* San Francisco: Jossey-Bass.

39. DuFour, R., and Eaker, R. 2002. *Getting Started: Reculturing Schools to Become Professional Learning Communities.* Bloomington, IL: National Education Service.

40. DuFour, R. 2003. "Building a Professional Learning Community." *The School Administrator.* May.

41. Senge, P. 1996. "The Ecology of Leadership." *Leader to Leader* 2, Fall. Available from: http://www.pfdf.org/leaderbooks/L2L/fall96/senge.html.

42. Reeves, D. 2003. "Leadership and Learning: The Role of System Leadership." *Focus on Achievement* 4, no. 3 (February).

43. Tompkins, R. 2003. "Leaving Rural Children Behind." *Education Week.* March 26.

44. King, John. 2004. "Paige Calls NEA 'Terrorist Organization'." Posted February 23. Cited 17 May 2004. Available from: *http://www.cnn.com/2004/EDUCATION/02/23/paige.terrorist.nea.*

45. Piana, L. 1999. "Reading, Writing, Race, and Resegregation: 45 Years After *Brown v. Board of Education.*" *ColorLines* 2, no. X (Spring).

46. Gordon, R. 1999. "Language Hysteria: The Aftermath of California's Bilingual Ban—*An Interview with Deborah Escobedo.*" *ColorLines.* Spring. Available from: *http://www.arg.org/C-Lines/CLArchive/story2_1_04.html.*

47. Digitale, R. 2004. "SR Schools' Bilingual Policy Questioned." *The Press Democrat.* May 11.

48. Mukhopadhyay, C., R. and Henze. 2003. "Using Anthropology to Make Sense of Human Diversity." *Phi Delta Kappan* 84, no. 9 (May): 669–78.

49. Lewis-Charp, H. 2003. "Breaking the Silence: White Students' Perspectives on Race and Multiracial Schools." *Phi Delta Kappan* 85, no. 4 (December): 279–85.

50. Polite, L., and E. Saenger. . 2003. "A Pernicious Silence: Confronting Race in the Elementary Classroom." *Phi Delta Kappan* 85, no. 4 (December): 274–78.

51. Lewis-Charp, 2003. See note 49.

52–56. Various Contributors. 2004. "Beyond Black, White, and *Brown.*" Cited 20 May 2004. Available from: *http://www.thenation.com/doc.mhtml?i=20040503&c=1&s=forum.* Specific authors quoted: Pedro Naguera, Frank Wu, Asa Hilliard III, Jonathan Kozol, Mari Matsuda.